A HISTORY OF
MULTICULTURAL AMERICA

The Westward Movement and Abolitionism

1815-1850

William Loren Katz

RSVP
RAINTREE
STECK-VAUGHN
P U B L I S H E R S
The Steck-Vaughn Company

Austin, Texas

For Laurie

Cover and interior design: Joyce Spicer
Electronic Production: Scott Melcer

Library of Congress Cataloging-in-Publication Data

Katz, William Loren.
   The westward movement and abolitionism, 1815-1850 / by
William Loren Katz.
      p.   cm. — (A History of multicultural America)
   Includes bibliographical references and index.
   Summary: A multicultural history of the United States, from 1815
to 1850, focusing on the first wave of immigration and the abolition-
ist and feminist movements.
   ISBN 0-8114-6276-5   —   ISBN 0-8114-2913-X (soft cover)
   1. United States — History — 1815-1861 — Juvenile literature.
2. United States — Emigration and immigration — History — 19th
century — Juvenile literature.   3. United States — Social conditions
— To 1865 — Juvenile literature.   4. Slavery — United States —
Anti-slavery movements — Juvenile literature.   [1. United States —
History — 1815-1861.   2. United States — Emigration and immigra-
tion — History — 19th century 3. United States — Social conditions
— To 1865.   4. Slavery — Anti-slavery movements.]   I. Title.   II.
Series.
E338.K28   1993
973.5—dc20   92-14965
                                                       CIP AC

Printed and bound in the United States of America

1 2 3 4 5 6 7 8 9 0 LB 98 97 96 95 94 93

Acknowledgments

All prints from the collection of the author, William L. Katz with the following exceptions: p. 20 Nevada State Historical Society, p. 29 Nebraska Historical Society, pp. 61, 66 California State Library, p. 69 Bancroft Library, UCLA, p. 70 Oregon Historical Society

Cover photographs: (inset) William Katz Collection; (map) Historical Pictures

TABLE OF CONTENTS

INTRODUCTION... 4

1　THE FIRST WAVE 6

2　IRISH IN THE CITY 10

3　THE ARRIVAL OF THE GERMANS....................15

4　THE MOUNTAIN MEN................................19

5　FROM MANY NATIONS TO THE WEST...............24

6　MOTHER TO EXILES..............................31

7　THE KNOW-NOTHINGS............................33

8　AN AGE OF INVENTION..........................36

9　THE WAR FOR FLORIDA 40

10　THE SOUTH AND SLAVERY 43

11　IN SOUTHERN CITIES............................48

12　NEW ORLEANS 51

13　THE WINNING OF TEXAS 56

14　EARLY CALIFORNIA 61

15　ON THE OREGON TRAIL..........................70

16　THE CRUSADE AGAINST SLAVERY 73

17　AMERICAN WOMEN BATTLE SLAVERY 76

18　WOMEN: THE FIGHT FOR EQUALITY 80

19　THE GREAT FOREMOTHERS 85

20　FROM ABOLITIONISM TO FEMINISM..............91

FURTHER READING.................................94

INDEX 95

INTRODUCTION

The history of the United States is the story of people of many backgrounds. A few became wealthy through their knowledge of science, industry, or banking. But it was ordinary people who most shaped the progress of this country and created our national heritage.

The American experience, however, has often been recounted in history books as the saga of powerful men—presidents and senators, merchants and industrialists. Schoolchildren were taught that the wisdom and patriotism of an elite created democracy and prosperity.

A truthful history of the United States has to do more than celebrate the contributions of the few. Ordinary Americans fought the Revolution that set this country free, and ordinary workers built the nation's economy. The overwhelming majority of people held no office, made little money, and worked hard all their lives.

Some groups, women and minorities in particular, had to vault legal barriers and public hostility in order to make their contributions to the American dream, only to find that school courses taught little about their achievements. The valiant struggle of minorities and women to win dignity, equality, and justice often was omitted from history's account. Some believe this omission was accidental or careless, others insist it was purposeful.

Native Americans struggled valiantly to survive military and cultural assaults on their lives. But the public was told Native Americans were savages undeserving of any rights to their land or culture. African Americans battled to break the chains of slavery and to scale the walls of racial discrimination. But a century after slavery ended, some textbooks still pictured African Americans as content under slavery and bewildered by freedom. Arrivals from Asia, Mexico, and the West Indies faced legal restrictions and sometimes violence. But the public was told that they were undeserving of a welcome because they took "American jobs," and some were "treacherous aliens."

Whether single, married, or mothers, women were portrayed as dependent on men and accepting of a lowly status. The record of their sturdy labors, enduring strengths, and their arduous struggle to achieve equality rarely found its way into classrooms. The version of American history that reached the public carried many prejudices. It often preferred farmers over urban workers, middle classes over working classes, rich over poor. Women and minorities became invisible, ineffective, or voiceless.

This distorted legacy also failed to mention the campaigns waged by minorities and women to attain human rights. Such efforts did not reflect glory on white male rulers and their unwillingness to extend democracy and opportunity to others.

This kind of history was not a trustworthy tale. It locked out entire races and impeded racial understanding. Not only was it unreliable, but for most students it was dull and boring.

Our history has to be truthful and complete. Our struggle to overcome the barriers of nature and obstacles made by humans is an inspiring story. This series of books seeks to explore the heroic efforts of minorities and women to find their place in the American dream.

William Loren Katz

C H A P T E R 1

THE FIRST WAVE

Immigration to the United States spurred national growth in the 19th century. Until 1820, so few people arrived that the government kept no record. By 1825, more than 10,000 were arriving yearly, and the government decided to keep records.

In the early 1800s travel by sea was a perilous undertaking on sailing ships. Voyages averaged 39 days from Liverpool, England, to the United States and 6 to 12 weeks from Bremen, Germany, which was the chief departure port for the continent. The cost of the trip was $15, and passengers had to provide their own food.

Peasants without land were told that in America land cost two or three dollars an acre. Swiss, Turks, Danes, Estonians, and Swedes headed toward Bremen. German jails and poorhouses were emptied to send people across to the New World.

Poor people were packed in the foul holds of ships without enough food and little space. The Atlantic rolled under them. Many died at sea. On the *Virginius* 496 passengers began a voyage in which 158 died, and 187 were seriously ill. The British ship *Larch* left Ireland with 408 immigrants and landed after 108 had died, and another 150 had become ill. When vessels sailed into American ports carrying a plague, ships were quarantined. The ill were returned to their home port.

Early government records show that in 1820 immigrants came from 32 nations from the Azores to Asia. Still most immigrants came from European countries and were men between the ages of 15 and 35 who traveled with groups of friends.

Farmers and merchants, physicians and teachers, miners and painters, printers and lawyers, sailors and seamstresses boarded the wooden, wind-driven sailing vessels. It was a time when women did not travel alone, so most arrived with their families. The new-comers spilled down gangplanks in the seaports of Boston, Philadelphia, Baltimore, New Orleans, and especially New York.

Some disembarked in Belfast, Maine, or at more than two dozen other small harbors along the Atlantic coast.

By the 1830s, yearly immigration was soaring. It passed 50,000 a year in the early 1840s then passed 100,000 a year. By the 1850s, it reached 300,000 a year and then 400,000 a year by 1854.

Efforts were made to modernize ocean travel. In 1840 Samuel Cunard, a Canadian, began the first steamship line. His passengers were at sea for only two weeks. But for most newcomers the voyage still took 33 days on the rocking Atlantic from England to America.

Immigrants leave England for America.

Many who made the trip were inspired by letters from kinfolk and friends who exaggerated their successes in America. Others were lured by dishonest travel agents who spun tales of easy wealth. Wisconsin launched a campaign to attract settlers. It published pamphlets extolling its virtues and riches in seven languages, advertised in eight European papers, and issued 10,000 pocket maps in English, German, and Norwegian.

Cities grew to accommodate the newcomers. New York City's population increased by 50 percent during each decade between 1840 and 1870, and Chicago doubled in residents in the same 30-year period. Of the 32,000,000 Americans living in the United States in 1860, four million had been born abroad. In Pittsburgh, New York, and Chicago half the population was foreign born, and in St. Louis it was 60 percent.

Immigrants from many countries helped build the nation's early economic and social institutions. In 1842 in Vincennes, Indiana, Adam Gimbel opened a department store. In 1852 Czechs in Milwaukee published a paper in German for 250 Czech families. St. Louis soon had a first Czech Catholic church named after Saint Jan Nepomucky .

Arrivals from Greece were few, but in 1857 Spyros Bazanos began *Peleponnesus*, the first Greek restaurant in New York. By then Nicholas Pappas had become the first Greek settler in Chicago.

For most migrants the first needs were a job and a home. Many settled within walking distance of their work. Old buildings were swiftly divided into tiny apartments. Families piled into hastily constructed wood shanties in narrow yards behind other houses.

Life was a challenge that some met with great ambition. In 1851

Frank Brodsky, a Czech, arrived. He could not find a job in New York City and did not have enough money for secondhand shoes. Each morning he began his search for work by blackening his feet with shoe polish to give the impression he was wearing shoes. Brodsky later became a wealthy businessman. Few were as successful as Brodsky.

The new arrivals often sought neighborhoods populated by people who spoke their language, reminded them of their homeland, went to their churches, and cooked familiar foods. As homesick people, they searched out the sounds and tastes they remembered. This was one reason they were willing to live crammed in with relatives or in old buildings about to be torn down for offices or businesses.

Cities were growing too fast to accommodate everyone, and city services were few. Newcomers had to help one another. The easiest way was for those from a region or town in the Old World to settle among their relatives or old friends in America. From this development grew ghettoes. From the outset ghetto residents had to depend on their own resources.

The first institutions Europeans built were religious. In 1860 New York City's 40,000 Jews were divided into 77 congregations because Jews from Spain and Portugal saw the Hebrew religion differently than those from Central Europe. As early as 1822, Mordecai Noah, a Jew, was elected sheriff of New York City.

In a generation or two European immigrants formed secular, self-help groups, often to help those who had just arrived, just as African Americans had done before them in the 1780s. In 1843 B'nai B'rith, the first Jewish American fraternal club in the world, was born in New York. In 1850 Czech Americans began a benevolent and educational society in New York City that lasted two years. Irish Americans also formed several societies to help other Irish immigrants.

Newcomers were sustained by a faith that their perilous voyage had not been in vain and that they would find America's promise. After all, they had arrived in a growing republic where ordinary people could lift themselves out of poverty.

People found solace in family, church, and tavern, and among other people like themselves. The first line of defense against despair was the family, its comforting arms and its enduring strength. Families also served as a first and reliable source of job information and contacts. Immigrants never forgot those left behind. Many newcomers sent part of their wages across the oceans. This cash eased family debts and pain and paid for passage to America for others.

Crowded ghetto neighborhoods generated a spontaneous sharing of life's miseries and successes. Up the stairwells of dank buildings floated the news of joy or sorrow, and down the stairs rushed talkative neighbors who were always ready to give comfort with big hugs or shoulders to cry on.

African Americans in Northern Cities

By 1860, a quarter of a million free African Americans lived in the states of the North and West. They were not slaves, wrote abolitionist Gerret Smith, but they enjoyed few human rights:

Even the noblest black is denied that which is free to the vilest white. The omnibus, the car, the ballot-box, the jury box, the halls of legislation, the public lands, the school, the church, the lecture room, the social circle, the table, are all either absolutely or virtually denied to him.

Some Blacks managed to become doctors, lawyers, teachers and start businesses. Many never forgot their link with those relatives and friends still enslaved. "We are awakened, as never before to the fact that if Slavery and caste are to be removed from the land, we must remove them, and. . . the moving power rests with us," said Dr. James McCune Smith, a member of New York City's black middle class.

To combat slavery and the "Black Laws" that restricted their lives as free people, African Americans in the North held state conventions, began newspapers, and circulated petitions. A black New Yorker urged nonviolent resistance to the bigotry imposed on African Americans who tried to attend white churches:

Stand in the aisles, and rather worship God on your feet than become a party to your own degradation. You must shame your oppressors, and wear out prejudice by this holy policy.

Others engaged in dramatic acts of nonviolence. Frederick Douglass, a former slave, tried to desegregate New England trains by refusing to move from the white section until dragged off. Former slave Reverend James W. Pennington refused to move from the white section of a Manhattan 6th Avenue streetcar. During the Civil War, Sojourner Truth, a former New York slave, tried to desegregate Washington, D.C., streetcars by refusing to take a seat in the "colored" section. ∎

C H A P T E R   2

IRISH IN THE CITY

The first large-scale migration to the United States from any nation other than England began in Ireland in 1845. In five years more than a million Irish men and women braved the stormy Atlantic to reach America.

A great potato famine struck Ireland during this five-year period. People in Ireland survived by cooking grass and seaweed. They also had to endure unemployment, low wages, and high rents. Though Catholics, citizens of Ireland had to pay taxes which the English rulers used to support the British Anglican church.

America tried to ease the famine by sending relief ships loaded with corn to Ireland. The corn was boiled and served in great pots in Dublin and other cities. This charity stimulated interest in the generous country overseas.

The Irish immigrants who survived the crossing to America, often faced new troubles in their new home. The first friendly face to greet them might have been that of a "runner," a man who wore a green tie and a shamrock in his hat and spoke with a thick Irish brogue. "Runners" sold the newcomers $8 railroad tickets for $70 and guided them to boarding houses that overcharged. Many newcomers lost any money they had brought with them to these unscrupulous characters.

To protect those who crossed the Atlantic, the U.S. Immigration Commission opened a huge immigrant processing center at Castle Garden in New York Harbor in 1855. Arrival was eased, and newcomers were better protected from "runners."

The Irish immigrants were also aided by newly established self-help groups such as the Hibernian Society and the Irish Emigrant Society. They began to publish booklets that warned the newcomers of the "runners."

Most Irish immigrants came as farm laborers from rural areas. In America they did not necessarily seek a rural life, but rather a new setting among others from their regions in Ireland. Besides they were unfamiliar with American farming methods. Most major U.S. cities soon had hundreds or often thousands of Irish families. In New York City by 1860 one in four people was Irish American.

Women from Ireland took jobs as cooks, servants, and house cleaners. Many became hardworking "serving girls" in New England homes, laboring for room and board and $6 a month salary. The "Irish servant" became a fixture in rich northern families much as the black slave was a fixture in southern mansions.

Young Irish American men faced a different set of choices. With pick and shovel, they were hired to build the bridges, roads, canals, and railroads that linked the new nation. Work was hard, and wages were low. Husbands and sons had to spend long months far away from family and friends.

To avoid paying those they had hired, unscrupulous contractors issued whiskey and tried to stir up fights on payday. Then the Irish were blamed for fighting. In 1853 the *Chicago Tribune* asked, "Why are the instigators and the ringleaders of our riots and tumults, in nine cases out of ten, Irishmen?" This kind of exaggeration gave birth to an early American stereotype — Irish men liked to fight.

The outdoor jobs of Irish Americans were often dangerous, and accidents injured or killed many fathers and sons. On railroads it was said, "an Irishman is buried under every tie." Neighborhoods of large cities, it was said, had many Irish men — but few with gray hair. Fathers died young, leaving large families in debt and economic trouble.

Women and men found better wages in America than in their homeland, but they also found prices were higher. They were pleased to be Americans, but they were almost as poor as before.

Irish Americans were confined to the lowest steps of the economic ladder. "No Irish Need Apply" signs barred them from good jobs, and they were denied promotions to better paying positions.

This increased the burden on each member of the family. Children had to pitch in. Boys of five or six sold papers or ran errands. Irish American boys and girls often took full-time jobs when they were only 13 years old.

In cities such as Philadelphia, New York, and Boston the Irish slums were the most congested. In the 1840s Boston had eliminated

"Five Points" was a New York City working class neighborhood Irish Americans shared with many other ethnic groups.

smallpox, but the disease arose again in Irish American neighborhoods. By 1850, one death was recorded on Broad Street for every 17 Irish American residents. A cholera epidemic cut through Irish sections of Philadelphia, New York, and Boston in the 1850s.

What sustained the Irish Americans during their decades of poverty? People were nurtured by strong families and a dedicated Roman Catholic church.

Families scrimped and saved to educate their children. Poor Irish American families also sent millions of dollars back to Ireland.

The Capture of Tammany

In 1817 New York City's leading political organization, Tammany Hall, did not allow Irish members. That spring 200 Irish American businessmen and laborers challenged Tammany's policy. Words were exchanged, and polite protest turned loud, fervent, and angry. Chairs and table legs pounded home political points. Windows were smashed, noses were punched, and men lay unconscious on the floor. Members of Tammany Hall summoned help from local taverns to rout the Irish who were challenging their authority.

The Irish Americans were not finished. In 1821 New York abolished property qualifications for voting, and soon immigration from Ireland began to rise. When tens of thousands of Irish American voters stood ballot in hand, Tammany changed its mind. Three decades after that noisy night of broken noses in 1817, Irish Americans dominated Tammany Hall. ■

Irish American neighborhoods celebrated festive occasions, such as St. Patrick's Day, with parades, dancing, and laughter. Women cooked Ireland's delicacies, and boys and girls took part in competitive games.

A restaurant along the New York docks had customers of many races and ethnic groups.

In a few decades, Irish parades featured men in the full-dress uniforms of local police and fire fighters. They were the heart of parades and the community's pride. Within two decades the lowly Irish immigrants had begun to climb the ladders of urban power.

Irish Catholics formed the first large-scale Catholic migration to America, which was a largely Protestant country. To Protestants, the Irish were "different." The Irish were Catholic, poor, usually unskilled, and unused to urban life. "Different" became interpreted as "dangerous."

Some Protestant leaders began to claim that Irish Americans would take over local governments, corrupt the public schools, and become a permanent lower class. To bigots, the Irish were the cutting edge of a vast Catholic conspiracy controlled by the pope. The American Irish became the first whites to face job discrimination. "Man Wanted, No Irish Need Apply" signs became common in urban centers. Some Irish Americans fought back with fists. Others responded in song:

Some think it a misfortune to be Christened Pat or Dan,
But to me it is an honor to be called an Irish man.

Irish Americans laid the tracks for railroads and hollowed out the canals. Then they brought their large families to settle near the canal banks or railroad lines. Men who built the railroad from Boston, Massachusetts, to Providence, Rhode Island, stayed on to become the first mill workers of Rhode Island. Their children entered public schools and went on to become clerks, police officers, councilmen, and mayors.

In many cities young Irish and African American men competed for low paying, dirty, and hard jobs. At times desperation led these young men to riot and bloodshed.

Some of both races tried to bridge the gulf. John Boyle O'Reilly, a Boston newspaper editor, asked his Irish readers to speak out against slavery and for equality for all. In turn African Americans, such as former slave Frederick Douglass, supported Ireland's effort to free itself from England. Douglass, who toured Ireland, was introduced to a crowd by Irish national hero Daniel O'Connell, as "the Black O'Connell of the United States."

O'Connell even tried to mobilize U.S. Irish against slavery. But it was hard to bridge the gap. Poor Irish American men had become resentful of ex-slaves, and they feared ending slavery would only mean more competition for jobs.

Congressman Mike Walsh of New York, elected in 1850, often spoke for poor Irish Americans. He pointed out that Americans had confined two peoples to the bottom of the economic ladder.

The only difference between the Negro slave of the South
and the white wage slave of the North is that the one has a
master without asking for him, and the other has to beg
for the privilege of becoming a slave. . . . The one is the
slave of an individual; the other is the slave of an
inexorable class.

As laboring men and women with a long political history in Ireland, Walsh's constituents supported democratic changes and were imbued with a nationalistic fervor. But they opposed any who would overturn the nation over a single issue such as slavery.

CHAPTER 3

THE ARRIVAL OF THE GERMANS

By the time the Civil War began in 1861, half of all Americans born abroad came from Germany. These German immigrants numbered more than 1,250,000. Some were rich, and some were poor; some were educated, and some were uneducated. They were Catholics, Jews, or Lutherans. Their migration climbed sharply between 1836 and 1845 and peaked in 1854 when 215,000 arrived.

At first economic opportunity in America motivated most Germans to move here. After 1830 and 1848 though, many others fled their homeland because efforts at democratic revolution in Germany had failed. Men who had spent time in German jails for their radical views were soon teaching in American colleges, although some well-educated Germans had to wield picks and shovels to earn a living.

Politically, the Germans in America first became Jacksonian Democrats and then, later on, Lincoln Republicans. Their views clashed with more traditional U.S. views on religion, politics, and slavery. Many exiles called themselves "freethinkers" and held radical views on religion. Some established utopian colonies in the Midwest and attempted to build their own idealistic communities. More traditional German Americans established little "Deutschlands" in Pennsylvania, Missouri, Illinois, and Ohio.

In Pennsylvania, German Americans rose to dominate state politics. Since the eighteenth century, the legislature had published its debates in German and English, and candidates for public office issued publicity in German and English. From 1787 to 1842 almost half of the state's governors were of German background.

In ten years German Americans became the second-largest Catholic group in the U.S. Only Irish Americans outnumbered them. By 1839, the states of Pennsylvania, Wisconsin, Indiana, and Ohio,

Many German Americans settled in New York City's 16th Ward.

all with large German-speaking populations, ruled that public schools had to teach in German when the demand was sufficient.

German Americans had an impact on many aspects of U.S. life. Some three out of four cabinetmakers and upholsterers in America were German immigrants. They earned a staggering $30 a year and their board. Some had been hired before their ships had landed. Unskilled Germans built the Illinois Central Railroad and then settled their families in towns along its tracks. Some 169,000 Germans crowded into New York City. They built twenty churches, fifty schools, ten bookstores, five printing companies, restaurants, a theater, and a library. German not English was the language that dominated business and social life in their neighborhoods. Second in numbers to the 203,000 Irish Americans, German Americans in the city were also blamed for a good part of the city's riotous behavior. For reasons of "personal cleanliness and regard for property," city landlords announced they preferred to rent to African Americans rather than either Germans or Irish Americans.

In the 1840s newcomers from Germany largely settled in the Midwest. Bellville, Illinois, had a German mayor, a German majority on the council, and boasted three papers in German and two in English. By 1852, Illinois elected Gustav Koerner as its lieutenant governor.

Hermann, Missouri, founded in 1837, was filled with scholarly Germans eager to be pioneers. They grew wine from local grapes and named streets after Mozart and Goethe.

German immigrants had earned a reputation for hard work, saving money, and becoming good citizens. German American farmers selected wooded areas for farms and did not mind the extra work of uprooting trees. They had come to build and stay, not sell and move.

By 1850, the German political influence on American institutions was pronounced. Refugees from the 1848 revolution in Germany — called "48ers" — brought a commitment to democratic values. At first most dreamed of the day when they would carry their banners back home in triumph. But within a decade many decided to remain and to help keep this republic the land of the free. Two German immigrants wrote a book to suggest that the U.S. annex the world into an "American Empire that is at the same time a Democracy."

The German people were great readers, and many talented editors and writers emigrated to America. By 1860, a total of 250 German language papers and journals had appeared in the United States. This far exceeded the number of any other group.

German immigrant workers also played a substantial role in early American trade unions. New York's Upholsterers Union included French Canadian, Irish, English, and German immigrants. In New York's Tailors Union German newcomers mixed with earlier European settlers.

Some German American unionists sought to strengthen the union movement. In 1850 Wilhelm Weitling published the *Republic of the Working Men* and helped unite German American unions in a New York Central Committee of the United Trades. That December Weitling unified German unions from Newark, New Jersey, to St. Louis in a Workingmen's League. In 1853 Joseph Wedemeyer, a friend of Communism's founder, Karl Marx, united German and other unionists in the American Labor Union. Wedemeyer became the first to call for the unionization of U.S. unskilled laborers. His union also introduced the idea that state legislatures should be influenced to pass pro-labor laws. This union welcomed skilled or unskilled women and men of every race.

In 1854 Wedemeyer and other German American 48ers wrote a radical "Louisville Platform." It not only called for abolition of slavery but demanded voting rights for women and African Americans. In 1857 Wedemeyer helped form the first Communist club in New York City. It recognized "the complete equality of all men no matter of what color or sex."

One of the first to enlist in the Civil War, Wedemeyer also recruited a German American regiment. President Lincoln made him commander of the St. Louis military district.

German immigrants spread to Milwaukee, which soon after its incorporation in 1846, had 40,000 Lutheran and Catholic Germans. Within a decade Milwaukee became the center of what some called a "new Germany." It boasted German singing and debating societies, theaters, symphonies, and an opera. Its breweries produced fine German beer.

Some Protestant Americans resented German American beer-drinking celebrations. On Sundays German Americans moved between church services and taverns. A religious holiday devoted to singing, dancing, drinking, and eating offended some people.

Germans brought a host of innovations to major U.S. holidays. Christmas had been celebrated with heavy drinking and pranks now associated with Halloween. German Americans turned it into a day of quiet religious reflection. They also introduced Santa Claus, the Christmas tree, cakes, and songs. They brought forth the idea of making New Year's a joyous observance.

Southern slaveholders were infuriated by the many German Americans who lived in the South but vigorously opposed slavery and advocated racial justice. German American intellectuals fired back. Some expressed contempt for other Americans whom they considered culturally barbaric or just dull. Some announced that many Protestant Americans were politically backward.

CHAPTER 4

THE MOUNTAIN MEN

In the early decades of the new nation, a breed of tough Americans plunged into frontier territories that were the exclusive domain of Native Americans. This group numbered about 600, came from many European nations, and were of every color.

These "mountain men" traded and usually lived at peace with those whose forests, fields, and streams they shared. From Indians they learned survival skills, to sense danger in the snap of a twig, the sudden rustle of a bird, or the crunch of leaves.

In the 1820s the mountain men began to rendezvous at the end of the "spring hunt" at Henry's Fork (in present-day Ohio) of the Green River. There an advancing European frontier encountered retreating Native American civilizations.

The grisly, bearded mountain men in buckskins looked more like the animals they stalked or trapped than men. Some, such as Canadian John McLoughlin, were great hulks of men. Others were short, wiry, and intense and moved with great agility. The trinkets, liquor, guns, and European glitter brought by the traders helped undermine Native American life.

By the 1840s, the frontiersmen had overplayed their hand. They had exhausted the land of its best furs, and some had antagonized their Indian hosts with their brash, greedy business methods.

But the mountain men had also paved the way for those who followed. They had charted the South Pass, the Snake River Route to Oregon, the Humboldt River Trail to California, and the Gila River Road to the Southwest.

To eager European pioneers in St. Louis and points east, these intrepid explorers delivered news of good grazing land and fertile fields. From them eager pioneer families learned where to settle, farm, and prosper.

French Canadian mountain man sketched by Frederick Remington.

Some mountain men became legends: Daniel Boone, Davy Crockett, Jedidiah S. Smith, Kit Carson, Jim Bowie, and Jim Bridger. But others hacked through many a wilderness trail only to fade when the frontier's story was written into books.

In 1816 Thomas Fitzpatrick, at age 17 and born in Ireland, arrived in America. The adventurous lad moved to St. Louis where he joined trailblazing expeditions by Colonel William Henry Ashley and Jedidiah S. Smith. Fitzpatrick located the primary land passage to the Pacific and Oregon. He taught Kit Carson frontier skills. Later he became a part owner of the huge Rocky Mountain Fur Company.

In 1841 Fitzpatrick piloted the first immigrant wagon train bound for California. The next year he led the first pioneer wagons rolling toward Oregon. He became a guide for pathfinder John Frémont and General Stephen Kearny. Unlike many Europeans who followed in his footsteps, he was known for being evenhanded and fair with Native Americans.

James Beckwourth

A host of other intrepid men had preceded him from Ireland to the American wilderness. John Lewis led the earliest settlers into the Shenandoah Valley. Michael and Nicholas MacDonald plunged northward into upper New York and settled at Ballston Lake. James McBride teamed up with Daniel Boone. Hugh McGarry in 1790 built the first European home in what is now Oklahoma. The Creighton brothers explored Nebraska, helped make Omaha prosperous, and founded a Nebraska college that bears their name.

Some explorers were as well known as Daniel Boone and Davy Crockett. But others, though respected in their day, were left out of the pages of history. In 1860 a journalist called African American Jim Beckwourth, born in 1798, "the most famous Indian fighter of his generation." But Beckwourth was lost to future generations when he was dropped from the chronicles of the frontier.

In 1823 and 1824 Beckwourth joined Colonel Ashley's Rocky Mountain Fur Company expeditions. He became a chief in both the Crow and the Blackfoot nations. After years of Native American life, he left to fight in California's Bear Flag Revolt and in the war with Mexico. In California, he served as a scout for General Stephen Kearny and pathfinder John Frémont.

In 1850 Beckwourth made a discovery that entitled him to an honored place in the records of the West. He found a pass through the Sierra Nevada Mountains that soon became a vital highway for 49ers heading to the gold rush in California. In maps of California today, Beckwourth Pass near the Nevada line, and a nearby town and peak, still bear the explorer's name.

In 1856 Beckwourth collaborated with a newspaper reporter on his autobiography. It does not mention his African ancestry and includes a drawing that made him look like a grisly European mountain man.

George Bonga married a Chippewa woman.

Hollywood movies continued this omission. In 1951 Universal International produced the movie *Tomahawk*. The black frontiersman's part was played by Jack Oakie, a white actor. Audiences learned that Beckwourth was important but not that he was an African American.

Black men such as Beckwourth proved vital to the fur trade. Colonel James Stevenson of the American Bureau of Ethnology spent three decades living with Native Americans. In 1888 he wrote "the old fur trappers always got a Negro if possible to negotiate for them with the Indians, because of their 'pacifying effect.' They could manage them better than the white men, with less friction."

An important example of black frontiersmen was the Bonga family of Leech Lake, Minnesota. George and Pierre Bonga, born at wilderness outposts at the time of Jefferson's first administration, married Chippewas. George played a key role in U.S. Indian treaty negotiations. In 1837 he arranged a famous treaty with the Chippewas for Governor Lewis Cass of the Michigan Territory.

Men came from many European nations to explore the frontier. In 1823 six foot, spirited Giacomo Beltrami arrived from Italy. He lived an exciting life among Native Americans and explored uncharted lands. He made expeditions into Minnesota and may have been the first European to reach the northern source of the Mississippi River.

In 1824 Beltrami reached New Orleans where he wrote two books about his many adventures. Proudly American, he said: "The world is now America . . . you are the first actors in it . . . the compass which conducts us to the port or makes us run against the rocks." Beltrami returned to Europe where he became a well-known scholar.

In 1835 Alexander Bielski, a Polish American, spent two years conducting land surveys in Florida. He died as a captain in the Civil War, carrying the American flag at the head of his Union soldiers. When California joined the Union, another Polish American, Captain Casmir Bielawski, was its expert in land grants and real estate titles, a figure respected for his integrity and vast knowledge. Also in California, Peter Lassen, a Danish American, became an early explorer of the northwest. Mount Lassen in California bears his name.

Although European women did not reach frontier lands as explorers, some arrived with the first waves of pioneers. In 1814 English immigrant Jane Barnes, became the first white woman to settle on the Pacific coast. In 1836 Eliza Spalding, who was disabled, her husband, and another couple, left New York for the West. Mrs. Spalding became one of the first white women to cross the Rockies.

As the party headed toward Oregon, she became ill from eating buffalo meat but survived. For many years on the frontier, she taught religion and weaving to the Nez Percé nation.

Before the early European penetrations of the wilderness, Native American men and women were the original discoverers and pathfinders. Their adventures largely went unrecorded when Europeans put the frontier legacy into print.

Frontier Clergymen

Though they are not thought of as pathfinders, the brave efforts of a host of clergymen also helped tame the American wilderness. They touched people with their Christian purpose and left the frontier firmly in Christian hands. John Stewart, born in 1786 in Virginia to parentage that included Africans and Native Americans, joined the Methodist Episcopal church. After an almost fatal bout with tuberculosis, he became part of a Moravian mission to the Delawares and later worked among the Wyandots in Sandusky, Ohio. Because Stewart's conversions included important chieftains, he became the first successful frontier Methodist missionary. In 1819 the Methodist church based their first official Indian mission on his experience.

By the 1830s, the archbishopric of Zagreb had sent thousands of dollars from Croatia to propagate the faith in the U.S. In 1838 Father Josip Kundek arrived to work among Germans, Swiss, and Native Americans. In Indiana he built a Benedictine Abbey and helped found the towns of Jasper and Ferdinand.

Three Belgian ministers served western Indian nations. Father Croquet became the "Saint of Oregon," Archbishop Soghers, the "Apostle of Alaska," and Father De Smet who the Indians called "Black robe," served as a missionary among Native Americans from the Mississippi to the Rockies.

Frederic Baraga, a Slovene, arrived in 1830 to work with Ottawas and Chippewas. In Michigan he taught them agricultural skills and crafts, helped them build homes and churches, and encouraged them to accept European education.

Years later Louis Adamic, a Yugoslav American researcher, interviewed a Chippewa whose grandfather knew Baraga:

> My grandfather said Baraga was completely and always good to the Indians and really wished them well and tried to help them. He respected the Indians as human beings, respected our language, and customs. He stood up for our rights; he went to the governor of Michigan in our behalf, and to Washington. ■

CHAPTER 5

FROM MANY NATIONS TO THE WEST

Within the United States, pioneer men and women of every nationality, religion, and color headed westward to begin a new life. Some had recently landed from Europe, and others left homes in the East and South to reach the frontier. Most traveled in family groups. But each wagon train heading West included married men seeking land for their families and single men seeking land for their future families.

Swiss immigrants arrived early. By 1810, their settlement in Switzerland, Indiana, produced 2,400 gallons of wine a year. In 1831 there was a New Switzerland in southwestern Illinois. In 1845 a Swiss travel service helped 200 men and women reach New Glarus, Wisconsin, another Swiss American community.

In the 1840s, 20,000 immigrants from Holland landed on the Atlantic coast, and by 1847 some had moved inland and founded "Holland" on the shores of Lake Michigan. Another Dutch American congregation of 900 founded Pella on Iowa's central prairies. Father Theodorus Vanden Broek led 300 others to Wisconsin's Fox River valley to form a major Dutch Catholic colony.

Frisians from Holland also headed west. They took up residence in Vriesland, Michigan, in Pella, Iowa, and later in New Paris, Indiana. From Luxembourg immigrant families settled in Chicago, in the farming areas north of Milwaukee, and near Dubuque, Iowa. And from the Isle of Man 200 men and women interested in farming used the Erie Canal to reach northeastern Ohio.

Not everyone arrived in the West after crossing an ocean. Men and women from Mexico, and Central and South America walked or rode into Texas. Some sailed across the Gulf of Mexico to New Orleans or the Florida coast. In 1831 about 50 Cuban Americans lived in Key West where 16 craftsmen worked in a Cuban-owned cigar factory.

French-speaking men and women had been leaving their Canadian homes to cross into the United States since the American Revolution. In 1838, after a failed revolt against British authority, their exodus accelerated.

Most French Canadians settled in New England, Illinois, Michigan, and Wisconsin. They clung to their culture which was said to be "defined by language, determined by faith, and dedicated to the family." By 1839, those who settled in Burlington, Vermont, issued a newspaper, *La Patriote Canadienne*. French Canadians in Detroit in 1848 began La Fayette, and two years later those in New York City started St. Jean Baptiste, their first secular self-help societies. More French Canadians migrated southward during the 1850s on new railroad lines that sped passengers from Quebec to Boston, Portland, Maine, and New York.

Some frontier pioneer settlements were started by former slaves. In 1832 Virginian John Randolph's will freed his 385 slaves and granted them thousands of acres in Mercer County, Ohio. But the African American families arrived to find that Randolph's relatives had cheated them out of their land. In Piqua white neighbors raised money and provided jobs and comfort for this community of former slaves. African Americans responded warmly to this generosity. Most first settled in Piqua, then many left to make their own niche on the frontier. Some settled in Indiana.

Blacks, whites, and immigrants from many lands headed West in great caravans of wagons.

That same year another colony, the Roberts Settlement in Hamilton County, Indiana, was begun by North Carolina Cherokees, most of whom had African blood. Men and women built log houses, a church, and a school. By the Civil War, the Roberts Settlement had produced Black Cherokee doctors, teachers, and soldiers.

Other Blacks reached the frontier after escaping from bondage. Many found a warm welcome in a host of Native American villages where an Indian adoption system drew no color line. Many instances of intermarriage followed. Black Indian societies were reported in villages of New Jersey, New York, Delaware, Maryland, Virginia, North and South Carolina, Connecticut, Tennessee, and Massachusetts.

Scandinavians made up a large part of the western frontier migration. A mass exodus from Norway was initiated in 1821 by Norwegian "pathfinders" Cleng Peerson and Knud Eide. The two were sent to America by Norwegian Quakers seeking a refuge from intolerance. In 1825 at New York Harbor Peerson greeted 53 Norwegians who landed from the *Restauration*. They settled near Rochester on 40-acre land parcels they had purchased for $200 each.

Other Scandinavians settled in Wisconsin. Some Scandinavian newcomers built sod homes with dirt floors, 12 by 14 feet and 8 feet high. In their first years they had to endure burning summer heat and freezing winter cold. Snow drifts covered the tops of barns, so they had to string a wire to guide a man from his house to his barn.

Swedish immigrants passing through New York City and heading toward the frontier.

But there were also compensations. Norwegian Americans had bread every day and pork three times a week. "Here," rejoiced one pioneer, "even a tramp can enjoy a chicken dinner once in a while." In 1838 Hans Barlien wrote of the delights of his visit to Wisconsin:

> Now for the first time I am able to breathe freely. . . . No one is persecuted here because of his religious faith. . . . No restrictions are set upon freedom or occupation and everyone secures without hindrance the fruits of his own work.

Scandinavians continued to pour into the United States. Those from Norway paid $25 to $38 for a ship ticket and had to furnish their own food and bedding. By 1838, enough Scandinavians had landed in New York City that they launched their first paper, *Skandinavia*. In 1847 *Northern Lights* became the first Norwegian paper in the United States published in Wisconsin. It vigorously opposed slavery. Between 1850 and 1860 Norwegian Americans started eight papers, and six were in Wisconsin.

Some Scandinavians found their pioneers' dream in Texas. In 1853 S. M. Svensson and 50 settlers started a Norwegian colony near Waco, Texas. It increased to 105 settlers and became the most important Scandinavian American community in the state.

Swedish settlements in America increased sharply after 1840 when the Swedish parliament, faced with rising joblessness and a homeless population, ended a 70-year restriction on emigration. In 1845 Peter Cassel founded Iowa's first permanent 19th century Swedish American colony. It was proudly named New Sweden.

Swedish American carpenters, architects, and laborers and their families began to settle in Chicago. By 1860, the city became their cultural center, and Swedish was heard on its streets.

Early Swedish travelers in America were often led by Methodist ministers. In 1853 migrants paid $12 to $15, sometimes in the form of iron bars, to sail in steerage. So many crowded the home ports that an overflow left to sail from Hamburg, Germany. The

Danish immigrants listening to a Mormon preacher.

newcomers arrived with reputations for being hearty, pious, law-abiding people, strong-willed and hardworking.

Many Swedish immigrants were Lutherans, and they had more than 39 congregations and 17 preachers before the Civil War. The newcomers faced the pulls and pushes of their ancient ways and the new, demanding culture of America.

Some rapidly adjusted to the new life. Raphael Widen first became a successful businessman in New York and then Sweden's first pioneer in Illinois. By 1824, he had made himself a force in Illinois politics. He played a vital role in the legislative struggle that led to the banning of slavery in Illinois.

Swedish immigrants settled in states as widely separated as Minnesota, Virginia, and Texas. There were only 12 Swedes in Minnesota in 1850 but 12,000 Swedish Americans by 1860. Other arrivals from Sweden formed Stockholm, an immigrant town near Richmond, Virginia. Still others reached Brownsboro in northeastern Texas where they founded the "Normandy" settlement.

Hundreds of Danes left their country in the mid-1800s and sought homes in the Midwest. By 1845, Danish Americans had formed a farming community near Hartland, Wisconsin. Others developed in New Denmark, Neenah, and three other places in the state. Racine became the center of Danish culture in America and was called Dane City. Other Danish Americans chose to live among Norwegian Americans.

Many Danish immigrants were Mormons, including more than a dozen who came from Iceland. By 1860, many of these Mormons planned to live among their brethren in Utah.

Other Danish pioneers had built happy, new lives in Wisconsin, Iowa, Illinois, Minnesota, Nebraska, and the Dakotas. From Cedar Falls, Iowa, Christian Jensen wrote home to tell of his happy experiences in the republic and his plans for the future:

> Here is limitless forest land which can be bought for
> next to nothing. The Americans are honest people. The
> country is ruled by a president elected for 4 years. There
> are good civil courts and many pretty girls. I am going
> to marry one.

In 1850 Fredrika Bremer, Sweden's leading novelist visited

Minnesota. Her *Homes of the New World* stimulated increased Scandinavian immigration. Three years later she wrote of the hope she felt for her people in Minnesota:

> What a glorious new Scandinavia might not Minnesota become! Here would the Swede find again his clear, romantic lakes, the plains of Scandia rich in corn . . . . here would the Norwegian find his rapid rivers, his lofty mountains . . . and both nations their hunting fields and their fisheries. The Danes might here pasture their flocks and herds and lay out their farms on richer and less misty coasts than those of Denmark . . . .

Most Jews who came to America settled in large cities in the East, but some also became pioneers in new western urban centers. Laws in most European nations denied Jewish citizens the right to own land. This meant that few Jewish immigrants arrived with farming skills or a desire to become farmers. In 1817 Jews had lived in Cincinnati for two years before it was incorporated as a city. By 1824, the town had a Hebrew Congregation, and by 1860 about 10,000 American Jews called it home.

Julius Meyer and Standing Bear

By the Civil War, other Jewish Americans had become residents of Cleveland, Dayton, Akron, and Columbus, Ohio, and Chicago, Louisville, Milwaukee, Detroit, and Indianapolis. John and Augusta Levy were among the pioneer setters of La Crosse, Wisconsin, and bustling St. Louis had more than 50 Jews.

In Easton, Pennsylvania, early Jewish settlers became watchmakers, cattle dealers, shoemakers, middle-class merchants, and common laborers. The town boasted a Jewish American brewer, a teamster, a lawyer, and a boatman. And by the 1840s, Chicago had enough Jewish settlers to form a Congregation which they proudly called "The Congregation of the Men of the West."

For Jewish American families, the challenge of settling in new cities helped provoke a religious reform movement. By 1854, Cincinnati became the center for Reform Judaism. Its acknowledged leader, Rabbi Isaac Wise, was a prolific lecturer and writer. By

1843, he had a formidable opponent in Rabbi Isaac Leeser of Philadelphia who led the more traditional Spanish Jewish congregants. He opposed Wise's liberal teachings.

Other American Jews first arrived in frontier communities as peddlers. They sold various items of European culture — tools, fancy clothes, and household goods. Some, such as Julius Meyer of Omaha, Nebraska, traded with Native Americans. He learned the languages of the Huron, Chippewa, and Pottawatomie. In Wyoming Jewish American peddler Meyer Guggenheim and his sons turned to mining and smelting. More than a few pioneer communities have been named after Jewish pioneers: Levy, New Mexico; Altman, Colorado; Roseburg, Oregon; and Mt. Davidson, Nevada.

Jewish peddlers often began their American frontier sojourn with goods on their backs and then graduated to horse-drawn carts. Some made enough money to start their own major retail stores in New York such as Macy's, Gimbel's, and Bloomingdale's.

Throughout the West and back East, American Jews relied on each other and their communities for aid and often formed self-help groups. Other European pioneers did also. In 1854 Czech American butcher Hynek Vodicka, a "48er," met in a Ripon, Wisconsin, saloon with other laborers and artisans to form the Czecho-Slavic Benevolent Society. It became one of the oldest continuing benevolent societies in America.

At first the society asked members for fifty cents a month dues. It agreed to pay $2 a week to members who became ill, $20 toward funeral expenses for male members (only $10 for wives), and $5 a month pension to widows. Its bylaws became the first printed Czech language publication in America.

This society soon developed cultural, educational, theatrical, and choral groups and tried to combat juvenile delinquency. The St. Louis branch became the model for hundreds of future lodges. The help these groups provided spurred further Czech migration. By 1856, there was a Czech school in Kossuthtown, New York, and the first Czech play had been produced in Wisconsin. By 1860, about 10,000 Czech Americans were living in the U.S.

CHAPTER 6

MOTHER TO EXILES

America has always welcomed immigrants whose political views and associations drove them from their homelands. Early 19th century radicals, revolutionaries, liberals, and religious dissidents found sanctuary under the Stars and Stripes. European revolutions in 1830 were followed by political upheavals in 1848 in France, Italy, and throughout the huge Austro-Hungarian Empire. Political refugees, including 200 from Italy alone, found a haven in America. Italian patriot and general Giuseppe Garibaldi landed in the United States in 1850. He lived with a friend in Staten Island where he made his living by hunting, fishing, and making candles.

Upon arrival some pioneers demonstrated their pride in American liberty. In 1852 dozens of Germans landed in Boston. They marched across the city carrying a sign: "Hail Columbia, Land of the Free. We will be No Burden to Massachusetts." Then they boarded trains bound for the Midwest.

At first these political refugees called themselves exiles. They lived in cities where they met in taverns, restaurants, or homes to pound the political table. They vowed to liberate their motherland and return in triumph. Many launched journals to promote their creed and to keep the flame of liberation before other immigrants.

Khachadour Osnagyan, an Armenian, settled in New York City, graduated from City College, and became a journalist. He began a migration of Armenian students from Turkey. In 1851 his *The Sultan and His People* became the first book by an Armenian American. It exposed Turkey's persecution of its ethnic groups.

Some exiles saw freedom everywhere as indivisible. In 1832 Czech physician Antonin Dignowity arrived in New York. He embraced the fight against slavery here as he continued to fight for liberty for his homeland. To expose European bigotry before his fellow Americans in 1857 he wrote *Bohemia Under Austrian Despotism*.

In 1850 Hungarians founded the town of New Buda, Iowa. Their government dispatched agents to watch for subversive activity by Hungarian Americans. The next year Austro-Hungarian spies reported that 158 Hungarian "revolutionaries" lived in the U.S., including 69 in New York, 21 in Chicago, and 7 each in Boston and Philadelphia.

The flight of Hungarian exiles continued. Alexander Farkas de Boloni, who reached the U.S. in 1831, wrote a book in his native language extolling America's virtues. It spurred further migration. His volume also added heat to the continuing effort to overthrow the Austrian kings who ruled his motherland.

While European exiles found refuge in America, Native Americans were driven into exile after 1830 when President Andrew Jackson signed the Indian Removal Act. Over the next ten years 70,000 men, women, and children were exiled from their ancestral homelands to Oklahoma and Arkansas because whites wanted to settle their lands. Their forced march, the "Trail of Tears," was conducted by U.S. troops and led to the death of thousands.

In time most immigrant exiles thought less about going back. They were firmly attached to their ancestral countries, but the U.S. was now home. Exiles and their sons and daughters soon adopted American heroes. In the 1830s President Jackson and the Democrats were their saviors. Vojta Naprstek, a Czech law student who sought refuge here, became a freethinker who questioned government in the tradition of Sam Adams. Reformer Ernestine Rose, a Polish Jew, led the annual celebrations to honor Thomas Paine. Polish American Adam Gurowski modeled himself after abolitionist Senator Charles Sumner. By 1860, many Old World freedom-fighters had turned to the new Republican Party.

The "Trail of Tears" exiled thousands of Native Americans from their ancestral homelands.

CHAPTER 7

THE KNOW-NOTHINGS

The large-scale arrival of European Catholics from Ireland and Germany sometimes provoked fear, animosity, and bloodshed among some Americans. Antiforeign propaganda began to flood the land about a "Papish" (Catholic) plot to seize the government.

Schoolbooks reflected the bigotry. In New York City a school text, *An Irish Heart*, claimed "our country" was becoming "the common sewer of Ireland." Another text referred to "deceitful Catholics." Catholic protests soon led to these two volumes being scrapped. This prompted a new charge that the pope had sent in agents to control American education.

Irish American parents in Philadelphia gained the right to have schools use a Catholic and a Protestant Bible. But this decision was followed by a riot. The Irish American Third Ward in Philadelphia was invaded by a Protestant mob which burned 30 homes and two churches and left more than a dozen dead or injured. An eyewitness reported "heavy gloom over Philadelphia" and "the streets leading to Catholic churches being guarded by soldiers."

Hate toward Catholicism was fed by tales that babies were being born and executed in convents. The best-selling *Awful Disclosures of Maria Monk* claimed that nuns were forced by priests to have children.

These hysterical stories soon provoked more violence. In Charleston, Massachusetts, a Protestant mob stormed a convent to discover its secrets. Finding no secrets, rioters ransacked rooms and set the building ablaze.

By 1845, a secret society of anti-Catholic, anti-immigrant bigots was established. Since members answered all questions about their activities with the statement, "I know nothing!" the movement was soon called the "Know-Nothings."

The new group announced its preparations to combat papal rule in America, "the danger of foreign influence," and the "poisonous vices of European social systems." One of its slogans was, "The Negro is black outside, the Irishman is black inside."

In 1854 the Know-Nothings and others formed the American Party which sought to deny immigrants voting rights and make their naturalization as citizens harder. It elected nine governors, eight senators, and 104 congressmen.

"Be as we are, " was the American Party's message to foreigners, but the party's members in the federal and state governments passed no laws against foreigners or Catholics. In fact, the American Party in Massachusetts sponsored a public school system, increased women's rights, called for the abolishment of imprisonment for debt, and sponsored regulations making it more difficult for slave-chasers to seize fugitive slaves.

By the mid-1850s, Americans had become more concerned with the battle over slavery than with foreigners and Catholics in their midst, and interest in the Know-Nothings waned. In 1856 the American Party nominated former president Millard Fillmore as its candidate for the presidency. Fillmore received only eight electoral votes, and it became clear that the American Party and the Know-Nothings were losing their appeal. They soon faded from the American scene. The heroism of American minorities during the Civil War evaporated what was left of their propaganda.

A long standing bigotry toward Irish Americans is captured in this 1868 cartoon by Thomas Nast. Club over his head, his foot on a black man, is the stereotype of the Irishman on the left.

The Mormon Exodus

Although prejudice against Catholics rose and then fell, acts of hate against the Mormon church, founded by Joseph Smith in New York in 1830, were unrelenting for 30 years. When Smith led his followers to Missouri, they were already resented as antislavery forces. They kept to themselves but were soon attacked by mobs. "For the public good," said the governor, they "must be exterminated or driven from the state." Riots, several dozen violent deaths, and the arrest of Smith drove surviving Mormons to Carthage, Illinois. There, Smith and his brother were imprisoned by lawmen and then assassinated by a mob that raided the jail.

In 1847 Brigham Young led the Mormons to Salt Lake City, Utah. In their new home the Mormons successfully cared for the poor and built a strong communal economy. Their leaders demanded tightly controlled communities and unreserved obedience by members. Salvation, said the Mormon leadership, was for Mormons alone, and this infuriated many people. Outsiders saw the Mormon elite as dangerous and despotic.

Highly provocative to outsiders was the Mormon practice of multiple marriages for men (but not women). Foes saw this not as a religious practice but as a violation of basic morals. It led to legal battles and violent confrontations with infuriated mobs.

The Mormons built successful congregations and communal economies in Utah. They raised enough money to pay for the migration of 50,000 European members. Almost alone they developed the state of Utah. They managed to carry out their plans and to ignore the hostile comments of their neighbors. ■

Joseph and Hiram Smith are assassinated by a mob in Carthage, Illinois.

C H A P T E R 8

AN AGE OF INVENTION

In the decades before the Civil War, American genius began to produce the inventions needed by a modern nation. People of many lands and colors took part in this endeavor to save labor, increase transportation, and produce goods faster and cheaper. The devices created helped to accelerate industrial growth.

The innovative talent of Americans can be seen in the United States Patent Office's registration of new inventions. In the 1790s patents averaged 77 a year, but by 1850, they leaped to 993. In 1860 some 4,778 patents were granted to inventors. Some were useless or humorous. But others made travel, work, and life easier.

Cities had to solve the problems created by huge populations living in congested quarters. In 1775 Swede Hans Christiansen built the first water-pumping station in Bethlehem, Pennsylvania. In 1809 Dr. Antoine Sangrain de Vigni from France administered a smallpox vaccine in St. Louis. Vaccines reduced the fear that urban growth and crowding inevitably led to devastating plagues.

By the Civil War, New York City boasted over a million people, Philadelphia 566,000, Baltimore 212,000, Boston 178,000, and New Orleans 169,000. Catholics, who had numbered only 15,000 in 1815, now made up half the New York population.

Of the city's 32 Catholic parishes most were Irish American. These citizens played key roles in a growing New York. In 1784 Christopher Colles gave the state assembly his plan for a canal that would link the Great Lakes with New York City. Another son of Irish Americans, Robert Fulton, built the first commercially successful steamboat. His *Clermont* in 1807 sailed from New York City to Albany, 300 miles in 62 hours. Eventually, steamboats began to appear on the Connecticut, Potomac, Ohio, Mississippi, and Delaware rivers.

In 1825, after seven years of construction, the popular Irish American Governor DeWitt Clinton completed the Erie Canal. It ran

363 miles from the Hudson River at Albany to Buffalo on Lake Erie. Europe across the Atlantic now was linked by way of the Hudson and Great Lakes to New Orleans, the Mississippi, and the West.

The Erie Canal was part of the first widespread government road and canal program. Its success sparked further canal transportation projects from Boston to Baltimore. In turn, this led to further migration as people poured in from Europe to provide the labor for these giant projects.

The aims of the various canals were to link commercial centers together and bring commerce to remote frontiers. Another significant effect was that they helped to physically unite a nation three thousand miles wide from the Atlantic coast to the Pacific.

Recent arrivals to America made striking contributions to the new republic. English immigrant Samuel Slater fled his homeland in the 1790s carrying many valuable inventions in his memory. In New England he set up the first factories that relied on waterpower, and he also introduced machinery that turned raw cotton into cloth.

In 1831 American Scot Cyrus McCormick invented a reaper that cut six acres of wheat a day. Before McCormick's creation, wheat had to be harvested ten days after ripening. Since a farmer could only cut one acre each day, he planted very little. The new reaper revolutionized agriculture and helped develop the nation's breadbasket in the Midwest. By 1850, its creator had sold thousands of reapers and made more than a million dollars.

Americans from France developed devices that enhanced American life. In 1839 John Gorrie, born in Charleston to immigrants, tried to find a way to cool air in hospitals. He invented the first artificial ice making machine. By 1851, he had taken out the first patent on a mechanical refrigeration process that is the basis of refrigeration today. In 1850 Louis Bonard invented a machine for casting iron and later a loom for making hats. Samuel Kier developed an oil that could be used in lamps, greatly aiding work, reading, and safety at night.

Other innovative minds tried to make urban life easier. In 1854 in New York City, Elisha Otis, born in 1811 to English immigrants, exhibited his invention of the elevator. He patented it in 1861, the year he died. The Otis elevator forever revolutionized the design of buildings in New York City, the United States, and

The battle between the Monitor *and the* Merrimac *forever changed naval warfare.*

the world. Otis's invention paved the way for tall skyscrapers to be built.

Thomas Blanchard, of French English stock, came up with two devices that became crucial to growing American businesses. He created a wood-turning lathe, a machine that produced 500 tacks a minute, and another one that cut and folded envelopes.

John Ericsson, who arrived in the U.S. from Sweden in 1839, designed the first warship made of iron, the *Monitor*. He also created a 12-inch cannon and other military devices that made the *Monitor* a highly effective fighting ship. During the Civil War, the *Monitor* confronted the Confederate ironclad *Virginia*, formerly the *Merrimac*. For five hours shells bounced off both iron vessels until the *Virginia* headed back to Norfolk for repairs. World naval warfare changed for all times since it would never be safe again to use wooden ships.

Though their masters tried to deny their genius, enslaved Africans made important contributions in the field of invention. Their owners forbade them, however, the right to officially patent their devices. The Confederate Constitution in 1861 had a section granting masters ownership of any inventions by slaves.

Africans have been credited with bringing the zigzag fence to the Americas. Joe Anderson is said to have helped Cyrus McCormick develop his reaper. Another slave was said to have aided Eli Whitney when he created his cotton gin.

Benjamin Bradley was a slave when he made a steam-engine model out of a gun barrel, pewter, and round pieces of steel. He sold it and used the profits to build an engine large enough to propel a warship. He then was hired as an inventor at the U.S. Naval Academy.

Free people of color from New England to Texas also demonstrated innovative talent. Norbert Rillieux, born to an African mother and French father in New Orleans, was educated in Paris. At 24 he published scientific papers and taught in the French capital.

In 1846 in Louisiana, Rillieux invented a vacuum pan to refine sugar that revolutionized the entire industry. His device removed the water from the sugar and turned it into tiny white crystals. Rillieux also developed a plan for a sewage disposal system for New Orleans, but it was rejected. Believing this rejection was based on racial prejudice, he traveled to Paris where he lived out the rest of his life.

Other free men of color held patents on important inventions during the era of slavery. In the 1830s Henry Blair of Maryland held two patents on corn harvesters. James Forten, a wealthy Philadelphia manufacturer, created a device for managing sails on ships at sea. Henry Sigler of Galveston, Texas, created and patented an improved fishhook.

One black New England inventor created a small device that made the capture of whales easy and turned whaling into a major American industry. In New Bedford, Lewis Temple created a toggle harpoon that became standard for the whaling industry. One authority has called the Temple harpoon "the most important single invention in the whole history of whaling."

The Michelangelo of the U.S. Capitol

The early history of the United States of America marches through the Capitol building in Washington due to the skilled hands of Constantino Brumidi, who arrived from Italy in 1852.

On the ceilings of the Rotunda, 180 feet high, on almost 5,000 square feet, appear his breathtaking frescoes of American life. To paint his huge figures, Brumidi had to lie on his back atop a suspended cage.

"My one ambition and my daily prayer," Brumidi said, "is that I may live long enough to make beautiful the Capitol of the one Country in the world in which there is liberty." He began his great work on the Rotunda at 72, but after an accident, he died five months later, and others had to complete his amazing labor of love. ∎

Constantino Brumidi was photographed at the Capitol at work.

CHAPTER 9

THE WAR FOR FLORIDA

The longest and most successful slave resistance in American history was fought on the fertile peninsula of Florida in the years between the War of 1812 and the Civil War. For 42 years an intrepid force of Africans and Seminoles fought for their freedom and held the U.S. Army, Navy, and Marines at bay.

This Florida alliance began in the days before the American Revolution. Africans, early explorers of the peninsula, helped the Seminoles survive and live productively in Florida's tropical climate, high grass, and marshes. The two peoples of color formed an agricultural and military alliance.

To slave owners in Georgia and the Carolinas, Florida was a beacon of freedom that had to be extinguished. To achieve this goal, pro-slavery forces launched one invasion after another before the U.S. purchased Florida in 1819.

Escaped African slaves were early explorers of Florida.

Generations of Seminole families built homes and tried to live in peace. They raised abundant crops of vegetables, corn, sweet potatoes, and cotton, and they fished and hunted for game. Some owned large herds of cattle or horses. They brought up their children and cared for the elderly as free women and men.

Africans ran vast plantations that, according to U.S. military officials, stretched for 50 miles along the banks of the Apalachicola River. This life in Florida produced people that a white observer called "stout and even gigantic . . . the finest looking people I have ever seen."

However, the entire Seminole nation lived in fear that the giant nation to the North would seize their land. For African Seminoles, liberty itself was at stake. Because they knew that they would be returned to bondage if captured, Africans became the Seminoles' most determined fighters. As experts on European strengths and weakness, Africans also became Seminole leaders and advisors.

President James Madison had been giving slave-catching invasions of Florida his secret support. In retaliation for the incursions, African-led Seminoles destroyed a U.S. wagon train, bottled up a Georgia militia, and assassinated a local enemy figure. The president hastily withdrew his support.

In 1816 General Andrew Jackson ordered an invasion to end "this perpetual harbor for our slaves." Their target was "Fort Negro" built by Africans for the British on the Apalachicola River. At the end of the War of 1812, the British had left the fort, its four cannons, and huge ammunition depot in the hands of the Africans and Seminoles.

Fort Negro's commander was called Garcia, a tough, lean, intense man known for his cunning, courage, and cruelty. He held the loyalty of 300 men, women, and children. In July 1816, Garcia's forces at Fort Negro confronted a U.S. military armada.

U.S. General Edmund Gaines led a flotilla of U.S. warships, Army troops, and Creek mercenaries under Chief Macintosh. To taunt his foes, Garcia raised the British flag and then a defiant red flag. A delegation of Creeks sent to persuade Garcia to surrender were abused and sent back nursing some bruises.

The U.S. naval vessels opened fire. The eighth shot landed in Fort Negro's ammunition depot. The roaring explosion of gunpowder killed 270 and left only three uninjured. Garcia was executed, and the survivors were led back to bondage.

But the war against the Seminoles had just begun. Over the next four decades the U.S. spent $40,000,000 and sacrificed 1,600 soldiers to the Florida wars. At times half the U.S. Army was tied up in the peninsula. Almost a dozen U.S. generals using deception and overwhelming force, seized hostages but were unable to end the Seminole resistance.

From the outset of the Second Seminole War in 1835, U.S. officials were convinced that African members "exercised an almost controlling influence over" Seminoles and were "more desperate than Indians." In 1836 General Sidney T. Jesup concluded, "This, you may be assured, is a Negro and not an Indian war." It was both.

John Horse, chief of the Black Seminoles, in 1836.

Jesup's reports found "the two races . . . are identified in interests and feelings."

To divide and defeat the enemy, the U.S. violated flags of truce and seized women and children as hostages. To hold U.S. troops at bay, Seminoles developed guerrilla warfare techniques. Meanwhile, the Seminoles had the additional burden of moving their families out of harms' way. In June 1837, Jesup reported:

> We have at no former period in our history had to contend with so formidable an enemy. No Seminole proves false to his country, nor has a single instance ever occurred of a first-rate warrior having surrendered.

The warfare and negotiations continued on and off and were not concluded until 1858. U.S. generals wanted to make peace since they could not defeat the Seminole nation. But they were often caught between slaveholders who demanded the return of their "property" and Seminole leaders determined never to surrender their husbands, wives, and loved ones. By the time most Seminoles were removed to Oklahoma in 1858, the two peoples of color had virtually united.

Black Seminoles preserve ancient traditions in their marriage ceremony and dress.

THE SOUTH AND SLAVERY

The invention of the cotton gin in 1793 by Eli Whitney drove down the cost of making cotton by reducing the number of workers needed to pick out the seeds. As prices for cotton garments fell, new customers appeared. Southern plantations produced the raw cotton, and New England plants turned it into clothing. Cotton soon accounted for two-thirds of all American exports.

As cotton had become king so had slavery. Planters depended on African labor. A Georgia doctor admitted "without a population of blacks the whole country would become a desert." With demand rising, planters bought more land for cotton and more slaves to work the fields.

Slaves were sold in auctions to the highest bidder.

Masters of slaves became the dominant political leaders in southern states. The 3,000 richest slaveholders controlled the South's eight million whites and four million African Americans.

For slave families the cotton gin spelled tragedy. Once masters talked of liberating their slaves after years of service but no longer. They had become too valuable to set free.

Production and sale of cotton clothing rose, but the life span of the slave fell. Slaves became cogs in a giant machine that churned out cotton and profits for their owners. Men, women, and children as young as nine years old worked long hours in the hot sun. Attention was paid to their productivity and not their health and safety.

To insure their profits, owners tried to control every aspect of slave life. The laws of southern states forbid slaves to learn to read and write, and even imposed severe penalties for any white who taught them. Slaves had no right to raise a hand against a white person even in self-defense. They had no rights, only duties and obligations. "The slave, to remain a slave," ruled a North Carolina judge in 1829, "must be made sensible that there is no appeal from his master."

Some owners were kind, and others were not. But owners insisted on naming babies born to slaves and on renaming each person they bought. Masters had the right to decide if slaves could marry, attend Christian worship, or visit nearby relatives. Africans were dealt with merely as property. They could be lost at cards, given as presents, or rented out.

Moreover, the slave system was one of unending conflict. Africans had never surrendered their humanity or hope for freedom. They resisted their conditions as best they could.

The slaves' first line of defense was the family since it provided the love and courage necessary for survival. Powerful bonds of kinship and love had strengthened African life. In the New World these strong bonds furnished a protective shield and a nourishing warmth for individuals.

Slave families felt it was important to preserve ancient African customs and pass them on to their children. A respect for the elderly and care for the young marked the African American slave family. Parents sometimes demanded that an African model of discipline, stricter than the European, rule their children's lives.

In slave huts, the African legacy was secretly kept alive. Babies were named for dead or elderly kinfolk. Grandparents were consulted on babies' names. Mothers and fathers, uncles and aunts trained the young in morality, survival skills, and self-respect.

Slave resistance took many forms. When masters tried to sell their children, mothers hid them in the woods. When overseers tried to abuse young women, they and their mothers fought back. Slaves in the fields responded to difficult tasks by slowing down their work, breaking tools, and pretended to be ill, injured, or insane. Some men and women fled the plantations for the woods and did not return until their masters agreed to negotiate terms.

Masters and slaves carried on many battles over the meaning of Christianity and the Bible. Owners saw religion as a way to keep their slaves docile. But slaves grasped Christian symbols and used them to breathe strength into their daily struggles and lift their

Slave runaways Ann Wood and her young friends chase off slave hunters in 1855.

hopes. African Americans in chains created a spiritual music to celebrate their will to survive and to live in freedom.

In defiance of the law, slave adults and children secretly learned to read and write. In Baltimore, slave Frederick Douglass traded cookies with his white playmates for lessons in reading. In southern cities and plantation houses, white women secretly taught Blacks to read and write. African American women who could read and write also taught black children the same skills.

Chief Joseph Brant welcomed escaped slaves to his Mohawk nation.

At times resistance to slavery took more dangerous forms. The most common type of resistance was flight. Slaves fled to the woods, the North, the frontier, or southward to Florida. Some were able to join Native American nations. Since the time of Columbus, runaway slaves had founded their own settlements in dense swamps or high mountains.

Men and women fled in couples, alone, or in large groups. In 1826 a large number of people escaped to the North by ship during a Virginia celebration of the Declaration of Independence's 50th anniversary. In 1848 an Irish American college student, Patrick Doyle, tried to help 75 Kentucky slaves cross the Ohio River to freedom. They were caught, and three black leaders were executed. Doyle was given 20 years in jail.

Daring escapes marked the history of slavery. Remus and Patty fled a Battle, Alabama, plantation in 1836 only to be arrested and jailed in Montgomery. They escaped to Georgia and were once again

Henry "Box" Brown arrives safely in Philadelphia.

Joseph Cinque, an African, led a successful rebellion aboard a slave ship in 1839 and then had to win his freedom in a U.S. court before he could return to Africa.

recaptured in Columbus. Again they escaped and were never seen again.

Two men had themselves boxed and shipped to freedom. Henry Brown had a friend mail him in a large box from Richmond, Virginia, to Philadelphia's antislavery office. Though he traveled part of the way upside down, he survived to write a book of his adventures. William Jones survived 17 hours in a box shipped from Baltimore, Maryland, to freedom in Philadelphia.

Those who could not escape disrupted plantation life. They set fires, poisoned overseers, and pitted owners against overseers. One exasperated owner said, "I'm nearly worried to death with them — if I had a jail, I should lock them up every night."

Throughout the slavery era, owners also faced plots and armed rebellions. To suppress insurrections, masters kept guns and weapons locked away, spied on their slaves, and paid informers. Each slave was required to carry a signed pass when away from the plantation. Patrols roamed the countryside each night to seize and question African Americans out after dark.

Despite every precaution, about 250 plots and revolts marked the history of bondage in the United States. They were a last desperate effort to fight a system that denied a person's liberty, humanity, and dignity. Slaves revolted in southern cities and on plantations, from both kind and mean-spirited owners. In 1850 a planter told Swedish visitor Fredrika Bremer:

> People are becoming compelled to more justice and gentleness towards their slaves, for their own safety. I have known times here, when there was not a single planter who had a calm night's rest; they never lay down to sleep without a brace of loaded pistols at their side.

The four leading plots of the 19th century brought terrible visions of retribution to white Southerners. In 1800 slave Gabriel Prosser in Henrico County, Virginia, planned to lead an army of some 900 slaves in three columns to capture Richmond. He intended to spare Native Americans and

Quakers. But a sudden storm washed out the roads to the city, and the plot was betrayed. One of the conspirators told the court that sentenced him to death that he had only done for his people what George Washington had done for the people of the United States.

In 1811, 500 slaves in orderly columns picked up recruits on a 35-mile march from St. John the Baptist Parish to New Orleans. Federal troops and the local militia were summoned. They surrounded the rebels and crushed their bid for freedom.

Denmark Vesey was a slave who purchased his liberty with a lucky lottery ticket in 1822. He plotted with slaves and free African Americans to capture Charleston, South Carolina. If his plan failed, he thought his army of six to nine thousand could flee to the Caribbean or Africa. Vesey and his conspirators were arrested before the revolt was launched, and many were executed.

In 1831 in Southampton, Virginia, Nat Turner, a charismatic slave preacher, led a revolt that shook the South. Federal troops and the naval ships *Warren*, *Natchez*, and *Hampton* were rushed to the scene, and a roundup of rebels began. But Turner's revolt had already taken 67 white lives. Turner surrendered weeks later and was sentenced to death. He reminded his captors that Christ had been crucified and peacefully walked to the gallows. After the Turner rebellion, one slave owner admitted:

> I have not slept without anxiety in three months. Our nights
> are sometimes spent in listening to noises.

Many other slave plots kept the white South fearful and well armed. In 1860 British reporter William Henry Russell visited southern states. Slave owners told him, "Our servants are perfectly happy." Privately, he was told, "We are living on a volcano." By then, the volcano was about to erupt into the Civil War.

Nat Turner plans his rebellion.

CHAPTER 11

IN SOUTHERN CITIES

Most European immigrants before the Civil War settled either in northern cities or headed toward the western plains. But a steady stream of newcomers also found homes in southern cities. Together with African Americans these immigrants gave cities like Richmond, New Orleans, and Houston a distinctly American flavor.

Some newcomers swiftly rose to prominence. In 1801 David Emmanuel, a Jewish hero of the American Revolution, was elected governor of Georgia. When Georgetown University in Washington, D.C., became the first American Catholic college in 1815, Father John Grassi of Italy was its first president. In 1837 Augusta, Georgia, had an Italian American mayor, John Phinizz, who in 1811 had graduated from the University of Georgia. He became the first Italian American to govern a U.S. city.

History books have rarely detailed the story of southern Jews. However, before the Revolution, Charleston and Savannah had thriving Jewish American communities. By the Civil War, these communities were matched by those in New Orleans, Mobile, Augusta, Columbia, Macon, Richmond, St. Louis, Baltimore, Louisville, San Antonio, Galveston, and Houston.

Reform Judaism first flowered in Charleston, South Carolina, in 1824 when worshipers at Beth Elohim tried to streamline Judaism's orthodox practices. Ousted from the Congregation, they went on to establish a Reform synagogue. They received some important encouragement when Thomas Jefferson wrote to applaud their efforts as a wise and progressive undertaking.

Jewish American congregations were found in the upper South. By 1838, two Baltimore Congregations had formed, and by 1853 there were two others. In Richmond, Virginia, Polish Jews in America began a Congregation in 1856, and other Jewish Americans formed two others by the time the Civil War began five years later.

In St. Louis in 1836, Jewish American settlers rented a room to

Quakers, some in southern cities, helped slaves to escape to freedom.

conduct Hebrew services. Within three years, the city's Jews had established their own Congregation.

Louisville had a Jewish American community in 1832, a Congregation in 1842, and a synagogue in 1850. In 1856 Polish American Jews in the city decided to build a synagogue and conduct their own services.

James Pennington escaped slavery in 1849 and wrote the first history of his people.

While foreigners were welcomed in southern cities, the presence of free and slave African Americans in these same cites rattled whites. Of the half million free people of color in the United States before the Civil War, more than half lived in the South. Thousands of African Americans labored in cities, often alongside slaves, in a mixture that whites found troubling.

Slaves in southern cities, with or without help from their free brothers and sisters, battled for liberty. In July 1853, in Richmond, Virginia, John Scott and 22 other slaves marched on the mayor's office to speak up for 118 slaves who had been freed in a will. Scott wanted to know the facts so the 118 might return to "the home of our forefathers in Africa." Instead, the delegation was arrested. But Scott still insisted "we cannot be still until we get home to Africa."

Free people of color were often accused of fomenting slave discontent and aiding runaways. The charges were often true. Some African Americans who had learned to read and write would forge passes that made it easier for escapees to reach freedom in the North.

For slaveholders the very existence of free Blacks was a dangerous addition to a system built for two, slave and master. A white complained that their presence

> . . . excites our slaves, who continually have before their eyes persons of the same color . . . freed from the control of masters, working where they please, going whither they please.

The accomplishments of free African Americans undermined slavery. As skilled mechanics, architects, plant managers, poets, civil engineers, and even inventors, they disproved white claims about the inferiority of Africans. In Charleston, South Carolina, Daniel Payne began a school for African Americans with a broad curriculum: arithmetic, literature, science, chemistry, botany, zoology, astronomy, reading, writing, and geography. He led eager students on scientific expeditions to the woods to search for insects, reptiles, and plants. Dr. Payne achieved fame after the Civil War as a bishop in the African Methodist Episcopal Church and as the first African American college president.

In southern cities some whites tried to ease the burdens of slavery. In Norfolk, Margaret Douglass, a white woman, taught Kate, a slave, to read. She was arrested, and a court ruled: "No enlightened society can exist where such offenses go unpunished." The court sentenced Douglass to jail for "one of the vilest crimes that ever disgraced society."

Some cities provided a setting for secret schools. In Natchez, Mississippi, Milla Granson, a former slave, ran a school for 12 children that taught reading and writing between 11:00 P.M. and 2:00 A.M. She graduated hundreds, some of whom used their new skills to forge passes for slave runaways. In Savannah, Georgia, Mrs. Woodhouse and her daughter, Mary Jane, both free Blacks, ran a school for 25 children at a time. "We went every day about nine o'clock with our books wrapped in paper to prevent the police or white persons from seeing them," wrote one of her pupils, Susie King. Ms. King went on to become a nurse and teacher during the Civil War and later wrote a poignant autobiography.

CHAPTER 12

NEW ORLEANS

Perhaps no city in America's history, not even New York, could boast of so many races, ethnic groups, and religions, as could New Orleans. At the mouth of the Mississippi it was a gateway to the continent of North America.

The site of New Orleans was first settled by Native Americans. Before the American flag, those of Spain and France flew over the settlement. In 1722 its 100 bark huts thatched with leaves and huddled in a swamp became the capital of New France. Its population included enslaved African Americans.

European rule was often challenged. In 1729 the governor uncovered a plot uniting Africans and Chickasaws. Next he had to rush out troops to combat Chauchas Indians. Part of the defenses of New Orleans were later manned by Acadians, Canadian settlers of French descent who had left New Brunswick and Nova Scotia when the British asked for their allegiance to the British Crown after winning the region from France. Over the years Acadians became known as *Cajuns*.

By 1751, every second man in New Orleans was a soldier, and the city became famous for dazzling military uniforms. To hold down soldier rowdyism, France sent over women willing to marry the adventurers. It also supplied Jesuit priests to bless the growing number of European marriages at the garrison.

Beyond the city's gates, the Natchez, Chickasaw, and Yazoo nations reminded the European garrison of Native American power. Inside the city, political authority rested in the hands of "Creoles," French or Spanish families born in the New World. They strongly prohibited marriage with Africans or Indians.

However, New Orleans increasingly took on an African flavor. Once Congo Square located at Orleans and Rampart streets had been a ceremonial ground for Native Americans. Then it was stomped to dust on Saturday and Sunday nights by African slaves dancing to their large tom-toms. Here Christianity met voodoo religious rites.

By the beginning of the 19th century, it was no longer certain that Creole or Cajun ancestry proved pure European blood. Some people of color now lived as free men and women and mixed easily with the French and Spanish residents.

Half of the city's population was African, many from the West Indies. Portuguese sailors arrived, some to join the famous pirate, Jean Laffite, who was of French Jewish descent.

In 1803 control of New Orleans was transferred for the sixth time in 91 years. As part of the Louisiana Territory, New Orleans was purchased from France by President Thomas Jefferson. At four cents an acre, the city of 10,000 became part of the United States.

African dancers commanded great crowds at Congo Square.

The first American governor, William Claiborne, doubted if he would last 12 years in a land of slaves, royalists, Indians and foreigners. After his first year in office, he said:

> This city requires a strict police: the inhabitants are of various descriptions; many highly respectable, and some of them very degenerate.

Law and order were never entirely secure. When a sheriff and his posse tried to arrest a visiting Spanish official a few years later, 200 citizens met the sheriff and posse with drawn swords. The angry crowds withdrew only after U.S. troops were seen hurrying to the scene.

New Orleans was always a musical city that danced to an African tempo. Between 1806 and 1809, 4,000 Africans and 2,000 Europeans arrived from the Spanish West Indies. African rhythms were gently stirred into French and Spanish melodies. Citizens of all races tapped time to the new music.

French citizens founded an Opera House that hosted many European stars. By 1816, the presence of so many African American patrons of the opera led the Opera House management to set aside a segregated balcony for people of color.

Segregation was not the rule at the fancy dress annual balls where rich white men came to meet exotic women of color in stylish Paris gowns. No other city in the world could host such dances and their unique cast of characters.

In 1815 the Europeans, Indians, and Africans of the city stood by General Andrew Jackson as Americans when he defeated the British at New Orleans. From this stunning defeat came a new vision. "One purpose and one consummation," wrote one famous city historian, "made one people."

One of those wounded in 1815 was Private Judah Touro, the son of a rabbi. A successful businessman, Touro lay bleeding until a friend crawled across the battlefield and rescued him.

Touro rejoiced and dedicated himself to his city. New Orleans became a boomtown, and Touro contributed by building schools, synagogues, and orphan homes. He funded the first public library and helped Baptists build their church. Touro freed his slaves. Then, to the distress of his white neighbors, he provided them with an education and jobs.

New Orleans became a thriving port and commercial center, and by 1816, Jacques Villeré had become Louisiana's first Creole governor. Its multicultural life continued to expand. In 1827 French American students organized the first Mardi Gras celebration and opened it to all citizens.

Citizens of many nations aided the city. By the 1830s, hundreds of Croatian American businessmen and mechanics earned their living in New Orleans. In 1841 German Americans built a suburb called Lafayette. To dig a canal connecting the city with Lake Pontchartrain, hundreds of Irish immigrants slogged through a putrid swamp. Visiting Irish actor Tyrone Power found them living on "a pittance and a forlorn hope," and at the mercy of a contractor "who wrings profits from their blood."

Mardi Gras brought out strange costumes.

New Orleans city commerce was in many different hands. Virginians and Kentuckians ran the city's brokerage and commission concerns. American Scots and Irish dominated its import and export trading. Spaniards were the entrepreneurs of the small retail shops and taverns on every corner. French Americans owned many of its magazines and stores. People of color ran the city's many outdoor vegetable and fruit stands.

Luke Jurisich, an immigrant from Dalmatia, began an oyster business on the Mississippi Delta and soon hired other Dalmatians. By the 1840s, Serbian Americans, who arrived to assist the Dalmatians in the oyster and fishing industries, had a colony in New Orleans.

The city's intellectuals had to grasp other languages and cultures. Alexander Dimitry, whose Greek family had arrived in 1760, became the first English editor in 1845 of the French paper, New Orleans *Bee*. The next year James De Bow, descendant of French parents, began to publish his *Review*. It became one of the South's most influential journals. In 1845 some of the city's educated people of color wrote and edited *Les Cenelles*, an anthology of French poetry.

An elderly immigrant in New Orleans from Sicily, Italy.

In 1847 Portuguese Americans started their first American society, the Lusitanian Portuguese Benevolent Association. By then, the city was also home to hundreds of Italian Americans from Sicily.

Freedom-fighters from Europe found a home in New Orleans, too. After their revolt against Austrian rule failed in 1848, 30 well-educated Hungarian families settled in the city. In 1852 they welcomed visiting Hungarian liberation hero, Louis Kossuth. A delegation of American French, Italians, Hungarians, Poles, and Germans greeted Kossuth in their mother tongues, and he responded in four different languages. By 1854, Greek American cotton merchants had formed a Greek Orthodox congregation.

By 1850, the city's Mississippi commerce grew to a hundred million dollars, and its population was 133,650. The first street pavements came, then the railroad and telegraph. Historian George Washington Cable recalled his childhood days:

> The city lengthened; it broadened; it lifted its head higher.
> The trowel rang everywhere on homemade brick and
> imported granite, and houses rose by hundreds. The Irish
> and Germans thronged down from the decks of
> immigrant ships at the rate of 30,000 a year.

The presence of so many foreigners may have heightened tensions between the free and slave population. Since colonial times, New Orleans officials had to wrestle with the problem of slave revolts.

City investigators found that whites and free Blacks aided slaves to gain passes, to escape, and to get arms. In 1853 a white teacher from Jamaica named Dyson and a slave named Albert were arrested, and they admitted belonging to a secret group of 100 whites and 2,500 slaves conspiring against slavery. When Albert was seized, he had a revolver and gunpowder.

But tension over slavery did not halt the city's mounting prosperity. By 1860, New Orleans' receipts from commerce were $324,000,000 per year. It became the Confederacy's leading port and was second only to New York City in the value of its commerce. Then in April 1862, New Orleans was captured by the Union fleet. When the U.S. flag again flew at Fort Parapet four miles north of New Orleans and Forts Jackson and Philip at the mouth of the Mississippi, master and slave relationships changed.

Owners said slaves, "would not work at all, and others wanted wages." The master of the Magnolia Plantation said his slaves had proclaimed they "will be free" and announced their intention to drive off or "hang their master." When they constructed a gallows, he fled. Slaves had discarded the chains of bondage to meet their former masters on a new, level field. New Orleans, pulsating, colorful, and diverse, had become a land of freedom for all.

These light-skinned African Americans served as officers in the New Orleans militia.

CHAPTER 13

THE WINNING OF TEXAS

Until 1821 Texas was a broad, sleepy province claimed by Spain but mostly inhabited by different groups of Indians, one of whom were the Tejas (Friends). A Spanish census of 1792 listed among its 1,600 nonnatives some 449 men and women of African ancestry. Those who were not slaves were able to enter skilled trades and professions and marry whom they chose.

American settlers arrived after 1821 when Moses and Stephen Austin negotiated rights for 300 U.S. migrants. Each American family was granted 177 acres with stock raisers given 4,428 acres.

Austin's first settlement included an Asian, Mrs. Kian Long, a slave of Mrs. James Long. At Brazoria these two women became good friends and opened a boardinghouse for new arrivals.

By 1832, European adventurers and more than 20,000 Americans had settled on fertile land bordering the Brazos, Bernard, and Colorado rivers. German Americans formed their own colony near Bastrop. Antonin Dignowity, a Czech American, came at the invitation of Sam Houston and was destined to be an inventor and doctor in San Antonio.

Some African Americans also found wealth on the plains of Texas. William Goyens, married to a white woman, began a blacksmith shop. But he made his fortune manufacturing wagons, hauling freight to Louisiana, and selling Texas land. After meeting with Austin in 1833, African American Aaron Ashworth agreed to set up his home in Texas. He became one of the wealthiest ranchers in the state and the owner of 2,570 head of cattle.

Mexican officials made the newcomers from the U.S. promise to become Catholics and not to bring in slaves. The Americans made the required promises but did not keep their word. Southerners who moved into Texas brought their slaves with them. Trouble between the Mexican government and the Texans grew as the Americans in Texas increased and became bolder.

In 1830 a Mexican army had tried and failed to expel the settlers. Two years later white Americans and a handful of Mexicans gathered to plan an independent Texas. Trouble escalated. In 1835, 30 Texans commanded by William Travis captured a garrison at Anahuac and defeated a Mexican army.

The Alamo

American Texans next seized the garrison at Goliad, the Alamo, and then the town of San Antonio. General Santa Anna's Mexican Army surrounded and eventually captured the Alamo. At about the same time 55 U.S. Texans and three Mexicans met at Washington-on-the-Brazos to announce formation of the Lone Star Republic. Mexico's leaders felt betrayed by the call for independence.

People of many backgrounds helped fight for the independence of Texas. Adolph Sterne, a Jewish immigrant, had long advocated that the United States annex Texas. When Texas became the Lone Star Republic, he served in both houses of its Congress. Samuel Isaacs, who arrived with Austin's pioneers, was one of many Jewish Americans who served in the Lone Star Republic's citizen army. Czech American Bedrich Lemsky fought at San Jacinto and then settled in Texas.

Free and enslaved African Americans also fought and died for the Lone Star Republic. Goyens, who spoke several Indian languages, was sent by Sam Houston to keep the Cherokees neutral. Two other slaves fought at the Alamo. Greenbury Logan fought on though his wounds left him severely disabled. Sam McCullough was the only Texan soldier severely wounded during the storming of Goliad. Hendrick Arnold led Lone Star fighters at San Antonio and Bexar where he was wounded. All were African Americans.

Independence was finally won at the Battle of San Jacinto where Santa Ana lost 600 men and the rebels only nine. After independence was won, some whites rose in the Lone Star's Congress to demand expulsion of all African Americans. However, Texan legislators commended their African American patriots and allowed them to remain.

The Lone Star Republic soon began to attract European immigrants. By 1840, several Czech American families had settled in Texas. One Czech, Bohumir Menzl, used his knowledge of botany and medicinal herbs to help settlers establish peaceful relations with Indians. In 1847 another 14 Czechs settled at Catspring in Austin County, and Czech American colonies soon sprouted in three other counties.

When Texas became the 28th state in the United States, war again erupted with Mexico. Czech American Cenek Paclt served heroically in the Mexican War and marched into Mexico City with the American forces. By 1854, more than a dozen Czech American families had settled in five Texas towns.

A Texas Jewish American, David Kaufman, who was wounded in the Mexican War, served in the House and Senate. He went on to represent Texas in the U.S. Congress and to give his name to Kaufman County.

About 56 Jewish Texans served the American cause, some in a regiment at Velasco, near Galveston. David de Leon, a doctor who twice led cavalry charges, became known as "the fighting doctor." In 1861 he resigned from the U.S. Army to become Surgeon General of the Confederacy.

Sam Houston chose as his surgeon general the Jewish patriot, Dr. Moses Levy. Isaac Lyons also served as a Texas Surgeon General.

Texans of German American descent also distinguished themselves in battle, some in special German regiments. One brave

A German American Agenda for Texas

During the conflict over Texas, some German Americans planned their own future. In 1839 New York's Germania Society announced plans to "Germanize" the Lone Star Republic from Galveston to Houston. A self-appointed pioneer in this effort, Henry Castro, was of Spanish, French, Jewish, and German stock. In 1841 President Sam Houston asked him to found Castroville with hundreds of Germans, Swiss, and Alsatians. Castro County and the town of Castroville near San Antonio bears his name.

Other German American settlements followed, one in 1845 in New Braunfels on the Guadalupe River. Then Baron von Meusebach signed a treaty with the Comanches in 1846 that allowed him to settle Fredericksburg along the Pedernales River. His colonists were poor but honest farmers with some criminals "sentenced to Texas" by German courts. ■

soldier, Louis Armistead, became a future Confederate general. General John A. Quitman, son of a German immigrant, who led a brigade at the Battle of Monterrey in Mexico, stormed Chapultepec where he became the first American to enter Mexico City's Grand Plaza.

However, the Mexican War became a conflict that seriously divided Americans. Congressman Abraham Lincoln challenged President James K. Polk's right to order U.S. troops onto Mexican land. Senator Thomas Corwin of Armenian and Hungarian parentage strongly denounced U.S. war aims as unjust. Ex-slave Frederick Douglass said the war stemmed from a desire for new land for slavery. Abolitionists such as Douglass feared that Texas might enter the Union as five additional slave states. Most Native Americans, African Americans, Mexican and Spanish Americans showed no desire to fight in a war to extend the domain of slavery.

American troops storm Chapultepec.

Resistance to the Mexican War also rose among enlisted men, half of whom were recent European immigrants. Some 9,207 U.S. servicemen deserted during the conflict.

Many Irish Catholics had joined the U.S. Army. But these soldiers became angry when U.S. troops in Mexico were urged or allowed to attack Catholic churches and priests. Dozens of these Irish American soldiers deserted and instead formed the *Los Patricos* battalion in the Mexican Army. The Los Patricos battalion was defeated at Churubusco when their ammunition ran out. But thankful Mexicans later erected a monument to their honor.

The war with Mexico touched more than Texas. A U.S. naval flotilla under Commodore John Sloat captured Monterey and declared Mexico's California province an American possession.

In what is now New Mexico American forces under General Stephen Kearny captured Santa Fe with little resistance. But Father Jose Antonio Martinez and Pablo Montoya organized guerrilla forces to continue the fight. Hostilities with Mexican forces finally ended when General Winfield Scott's troops captured Mexico City.

In the Treaty of Guadalupe Hidalgo in 1848, Mexico was forced to cede to the United States half of its land — the area that is now Texas, California, Arizona, New Mexico, Nevada, Colorado, Utah, and part of Wyoming — and was paid $15,000,000. In 1853 the U.S. government paid Mexico $10,000,000 more for land in what is now Arizona and New Mexico.

Mexicans who were absorbed by the U.S. were allowed to keep their language, land, and religion, and granted U.S. citizenship. Original Mexican land claims were to be respected by U.S. courts.

Mexican Americans freely practiced their Catholicism, but they lost other rights. White Americans in California seized Mexican lands, and U.S. courts rarely sided with the dispossessed. This system of unfair justice fostered years of bitterness.

The Poles Land at Galveston

In 1854 America's first large group of Polish immigrants landed in Galveston, Texas. Led by Father Leopold Moczygemba, a Franciscan monk, they carried plows, bedding, kitchen utensils, and a large cross. L. B. Russell, a frontier boy, later described the crowd that passed along his road that day in 1854.

The arrival of the colony was one of the most picturesque scenes in my boyhood. . . . There were some eight or nine hundred of them. They wore the costumes of the old country. Many of the women had what, at that time, was regarded as very short skirts, showing their limbs, two or three inches above the ankle. Some had on wooden shoes and, almost without exception, all wore broad-brimmed, low-crowned black felt hats, nothing like the hats worn in Texas. They also wore blue jackets of heavy woolen cloth, falling just below the waist and gathered in folds at the back with a band of the same material.

The Poles called their new community, Panny Maria. In time many Polish American families moved on to other places in Texas— San Antonio, Polonia, Bandera, Yorktown, St. Hedwig, and then Czestochowa and Kosciusko. ■

C H A P T E R   14

EARLY CALIFORNIA

The first Californians were about 350,000 Native Americans who lived in 105 societies and spoke six different languages and many dialects. The European explorers found them living a simple, structured life under chosen leaders. Their rituals recognized birth, death, and marriage with traditional dancing and ceremonies that lasted for days. Their musical instruments included flutes, whistles, drums, and mouth bows, and their young were trained in the traditions of their various societies.

The original inhabitants of northern California.

Over the years, the Native American population of California drastically decreased. Contact with European rule and diseases proved catastrophic. By the time of the California gold rush in 1849, only 100,000 natives lived in California. Ten years later only 30,000 survived.

A variety of people journeyed to early California. Initial Portuguese and Spanish explorations also included Africans. In 1815 the Spanish governor's cook at Monterey was Ah Nam from China. Immigrants from Dalmatia arrived in California as early as 1835. A Croatian missionary, Father Konsak, explored Baja California, founded San Antonio Real, and worked with Native Americans. In 1846 Mark Pulaski arrived from Poland and founded Pollasky in Fresno County. Later, as he built western railroads, he worked alongside people who came from Ireland, Scandinavia, Germany, and Greece.

Before the United States ruled California, its people of color filled every level of power. From 1845-1846, Governor Pio Pico became the last of 13 Mexican rulers of California. Born in 1801 at the San Gabriel Mission, Pico came from European, Native American, and African ancestry.

One of those who worked tirelessly to see the United States

William Leidesdorff

gain control of California was William Leidesdorff. Born in 1810 in the West Indies to a Danish father and African mother, he arrived in San Francisco in 1841 as captain of the 160-ton *Julia Ann*. He soon owned hundreds of city acres and became a prominent citizen.

In 1846 when U.S. troops landed, Leidesdorff's wishes came true. He was appointed a U.S. official. That year he also built San Francisco's first hotel. The next year he launched the first steamboat to sail in its famous bay. By then he was the wealthiest member of the city council.

In April 1848, when California's first public school opened, Leidesdorff was chairman of its board. But he contracted typhus and died a month later and was buried beneath the Mission Dolores.

By the time of Leidesdorff's death, the world was beginning to hear some exciting news from California. On land called "New Helvetia" owned by Swiss immigrant John Sutter, Native California laborers stumbled on pieces of bright yellow metal.

John Sutter

The gold rush of 1849 changed California forever. Gold had been discovered in California before 1849. In 1842 Francisco Lopez struck gold in the Santa Feliciana Canyon, 40 miles from Los Angeles. Three years later Captain Andres Castillero discovered a quicksilver mine. Also known as mercury, quicksilver became essential to the process that separated gold and silver from waste materials.

Before 1849, gold in southern California was first panned not by European Americans, but Native Americans. Then Chileans and

Joaquin Murrieta and American Justice

The treaty ending the Mexican war promised Mexicans who remained on their land the Constitutional rights of American citizens. But when it came to land grants and other rights, U.S. courts did not listen.

Mexican Americans soon learned they could not vote and had few political choices. When their protests failed to win democratic rights,

Joaquin Murrieta, a wealthy land-owner, formed an outlaw band. He sought justice for his people from a gun barrel, so Mexican communities shielded the outlaw from his pursuers. He was also secretly aided by the families of Jeremiah Fallon and Michael Murray, Irish Americans who sympathized with his fight for justice for Mexican Americans. ∎

Frémont: Explorer, Senator, General

Dashing John Charles Frémont, born of French Canadian parents, led early expeditions (1842-1844) into the Rockies and California. His intrepid band included such scouts as Kit Carson, Thomas Fitzpatrick, and a host of African American frontiersmen. In 1846 Frémont helped California's American residents establish their independent Bear Flag Republic. In 1850 two events redirected the explorer's thinking. First, gold was discovered on his land. Second, he was elected to the U.S. Senate. He became a famous Republican leader and then in 1856 its first presidential candidate. He lost the race to Democrat James Buchanan, but he had helped establish the Republican Party as the second most powerful political party in the land. In the Civil War Frémont became the first Union general to free slaves. Though his action subsequently was reversed by President Lincoln, Frémont had again been a pathfinder that many others, including the president, would eventually follow. ■

Peruvians from South America joined them. When U.S. gold seekers arrived after 1849, they encountered a poster written in Spanish: "It is time to unite: Frenchmen, Chileans, Peruvians, and Mexicans against the Americans."

In two years California's population soared to 100,000. By 1852, California was a state with 225,000 residents. Gold production soared to a yearly high of 80 million dollars. Some 100,000 California citizens now labeled themselves prospectors.

Gold fever struck people everywhere. Latvian sailors who landed in San Francisco stayed on to pan for gold. Russians left Alaska for California. Finnish sailors jumped Russian ships to escape service in the Crimean War and to find gold. Lithuanians left their homeland to dig for it, and one, Aleksander Holinskis, went on to write a book about his exciting life in California.

Slave owners traveled with their slaves, cattle, and supplies in huge caravans on the long trek from the southern states. Gold fever sometimes drove slave and master to pan gold together.

News reached the Scandinavian countries. Christian Poulsen, the first Norwegian American to reach the gold strike, sent home exciting reports that triggered a large Scandinavian migration. By 1860 California's population included 715 Norwegians, 327 Swedes, and 124 Danes.

Other Europeans headed for California. From France hundreds of citizens rushed to the state and formed more than a dozen gold-seeking companies. In Portugal citizens read dazzling eyewitness reports, and in response to these tales, Portuguese and Azorians migrated to California. Their numbers rose from 109 in 1850 to 1,560 a decade later.

Some Portuguese Americans began to strike it rich. By 1853, Jose Antonio owned 4,600 acres of Los Angeles real estate, and U.S. officials chose one of his buildings for their city hall. That same year Captain Antonio Mendez became the first person to navigate the Sacramento River.

The golden magnet drew many people from central Europe. By the 1850s, 50 Dalmatians lived on one San Francisco street. Lonely Croatian American gold seekers met and married Mexican and Irish American women. Other Croatians patiently waited until priests could arrange marriages for them in the homeland. Married Croatian American men labored hard to save enough cash to send for their wives.

Some 87 Austrian prospectors had landed in California. Half said they were also Czech. In 1851 Italy opened a consulate in San Francisco for its many citizens. By 1857, Frederico Biesta began to publish a paper for the 2,000 Italians who called the city their home.

California's daily *Alta* paper reported "the golden romance that has filled the world" was bringing in some of the best and worst from all over the world. It also attracted those who had already made names for themselves elsewhere, such as Hungarian American Augustus Haraszthy, who arrived in California in 1855. In 1842 Haraszthy and his family had founded Haraszthy, Wisconsin, now Sauk City. In 1844 he wrote a book about his American successes that inspired fellow Hungarians and stimulated interest in America. In California Haraszthy became a sheriff and then a legislator. Later he built the first successful wine plantation in California.

Members of many nationalities did more than hunt for gold. They established self-help and cultural institutions. By 1857, the first American Slavonic Mutual and Benevolent Society was formed in San Francisco. Its president in 1860, Vincent Gelcich, went on to serve in the Union army as a surgeon and colonel.

By 1849, a group of 40 American Jews who had reached San

Francisco celebrated Yom Kippur in a room over a store. By the next year, Jews had formed the Eureka Benevolent Society. They promised to keep in touch with and help each other. That April some Jewish American residents formed the Hebrew Congregation of Shearith Israel.

Jewish American prospectors contributed their lucky strikes to promote charitable and cultural advances for their people. Gold dust amounting to $4,000 was donated to purchase land for California's first Jewish cemetery.

Other contributions helped raise the $18,000 needed to build Emanu-El Synagogue in 1854. In 1860 a noted traveler, named I. J. Benjamin, called it, "the largest and richest in California and may well be included among the great Congregations of America." He also found Jewish American settlers who owned "great flocks of sheep and herds of cattle."

Some newcomers to the state played a role in its government. In 1850 Jewish American state legislator Elkan Heydenfeldt introduced a bill to ban gambling, but it failed to pass. The next year his brother, Solomon, was elected to the state supreme court. He joined another American Jew, Justice Henry Lyons, previously appointed by the legislature.

Some men became lucky, not by finding gold, but by finding customers in the goldfields. In 1849, 19-year-old peddler Levi Strauss arrived from New York by way of Cape Horn. In the mining camps where he sold tents, he heard men complain about clothing that tore easily. He decided to make denim and canvas pants with pockets strong enough to carry miners' tools. Levi's dungarees first appeared, and became so popular that by 1853, they were shipped in

A Levi-Strauss ad of the period selling new sturdy work clothes.

This California gambling casino and bar served all minorities including African Americans, Mexicans, and Chinese, as well as others.

Black miner at Auburn Ravine, 1852.

large numbers from his brothers' New York City factory.

Californians spoke in many accents, and the state's newspapers reflected the multiethnic character of the gold rush. In 1857 when John Xantus, a Hungarian American surveyor, reached San Francisco, he found seven English language papers, three in German, three in French, and two each in Spanish and Chinese. He missed an Italian paper and an African American one.

To the Chinese, California was *Gam Saan*, a "Gold Mountain," and it triggered a major Chinese migration. In 1851, 20,026 Chinese arrived, and almost all were men determined to strike it rich.

The Chinese wore blue blouses, wide pants, wooden shoes, and wide hats, and labored in gangs. Ship captains were taxed $5 to $10 by the state for each Chinese they imported. So these arrivals from Asia contributed 45 percent of California's annual taxes.

The Chinese came not to settle down but to find gold and return as rich men to their families. Immigrant Li Tang found neither gold nor luck. To his wife Mei Ling, Tang wrote some sad truths:

> The stories they told in China about picking up gold from the ground aren't true. We have to work very hard to get our gold. I work six days a week from when the sun rises until it goes down. My partner and I use a special wood box to mine the gold. One of us shovels dirt and gravel from the riverbed into the box. The other person rocks the box while pouring water in it. The water washes the dirt away, and the rocking separates the gold from the gravel. Most of the gold comes in the shape of tiny flakes and small nuggets.

Tang finally left California for Oregon where his luck was much better.

The sudden appearance of so many different people of color stirred dread in the hearts of many white Californians. At the state's constitutional convention in 1849, the longest debate focused on a proposal to deny African Americans the right to enter the state. It was narrowly defeated. But black people were denied the right to vote, hold office, serve in the militia, or testify in court.

Resistance to Injustice

To combat the "Foreign Miners Tax" and other discriminatory acts, people of color reacted in ways shaped by their dominant cultural traditions.

Chinese immigrants planned to rejoin their families. In the face of hostile attitudes and laws, they tended to their business. Foes, they were convinced, were barbarians not worth fighting.

After a decade of trying to ignore determined, violent Americans, they formed the "Six Companies," self-help groups based on China's six regions. What U.S. law failed to provide, these groups did. Their patrols brought law and order to Chinese American communities. For a yearly membership of a dollar, Six Companies officials ran schools, hospitals, and courts, and negotiated labor contracts.

African Americans adopted tactics they had learned as Americans. As sons and daughters of the American Revolution, they met hostility and injustice with petition drives, protest conventions, and boycotts. They started their own newspapers to protest bigotry and used the media to build alliances with whites.

To the California Black Laws that denied their rights to testify in court, vote or hold office, they reminded white Americans of "no taxation without representation."

In 1855 Mifflin Gibbs began a protest paper, *Mirror of the Times*, that was circulated in 30 counties. That year he and other African Americans initiated annual conventions to denounce slavery and demand repeal of the California Black Laws. Gibbs and others flooded the state legislature with petitions signed by hundreds of whites.

The African American campaign for justice did not succeed until the Civil War finally ended slavery. It was not that African Americans mounted a weak effort but that white bias was overwhelmingly strong even in the free states. ■

The governing whites insisted the gold fields "were preserved by nature for Americans only." In 1852 the legislature of California passed a special $4 tax on "foreign miners." This loose category included native Mexican Americans, African Americans, Chinese, Chileans, Peruvians, and other people of color, some of whom had lived in California before most white Americans arrived. For the next decade taxes collected from "foreign miners" paid most of the state's bills.

Some 2,000 African Americans as either slaves or free women and men arrived in California during the gold rush. Half listed themselves as miners. In San Francisco the new arrivals built a Mutual Benefit and Relief Society, three churches, and a two-story

Biddy Mason, California pioneer.

cultural center with a reading room and a library of 800 volumes.

In the goldfields, African Americans faced more than hostile laws. White prospectors spread the rumor that Africans had to be barred because they had "an antenna that enables them to detect gold." Blacks, of course, wished it was true.

Black gold seekers, like others, often had little luck, and some lost what they found. An African American named Dick took a thousand dollars in gold nuggets to the gambling tables and lost it in one night. He killed himself. But slaves such as Alvin Coffey and Daniel Rogers mined enough gold to purchase their families' freedom and begin new careers as free people in the state.

More than a few African Americans in California found their golden opportunities far from the diggings. In 1851 slave Biddy Mason walked all the way from Mississippi behind the 300-wagon caravan of her master. Her job was to care for her master's livestock. In California, with aid from a white sheriff, she emancipated herself and her three daughters. Mrs. Mason saved her money and invested

Yung Wing, Scholar

In 1847 Yung Wing arrived with two other Chinese students to begin his education in Massachusetts. After he graduated from Yale University, he found his purpose in life:

"Determined that the rising generation of China should enjoy the same educational advantages that I had enjoyed; that through western education China should be regenerated, become enlightened and powerful. To accomplish that object became the guiding star of my ambition. Toward such a goal I directed all my mental resources and energies. Through thick and thin, and the vicissitudes of a checkered life from 1854 to 1872 I labored and waited and waited for its consummation."

In 1874 Yung Wing's efforts bore fruit. Chinese students arrived in the United States to attend college. He became known as the father of the Chinese student movement in America. For China, he provided information on Western scientific methods.

Yung Wing worked to bring reform to China and bring about closer relations with the United States. He became the first Chinese American to become a naturalized citizen.

In 1902, when his political enemies in China put a price on his head, Wing fled to his new homeland. He died at 84 in 1912, the year his comrades in China finally overthrew the despotic Manchu Dynasty. ■

in Los Angeles real estate. She used her accumulated wealth to aid the less fortunate. When she found they were not accepted in white schools, Mrs. Mason began a school to train black women as nurses.

In California slaves found white and black hands willing to break their chains. White attorneys stood ready to defend slave run-aways in court. African American Mary Ellen Pleasant rode off to rural areas to rescue people illegally held. Once emancipation was won, she personally campaigned to desegregate San Francisco's horse-drawn streetcars.

California became the country's richest African American community. Blacks in California were teachers, editors, wagon drivers, and caterers as well as day laborers.

But even wealthy African Americans could be denied the right to attend white California schools. In 1845 black educator J.B. Sanderson arrived and opened schools for Blacks in Sacramento, Stockton, San Francisco, and Oakland. Hundreds of young males and females attended his pioneer classes.

Prejudice against Blacks continued even after California entered the Union as a free state in 1850. For Sarah Lester merely attending a white high school in 1858 triggered a confrontation. Few denied her brilliance. Ms. Lester at 15 was second highest in the school's academic achievement. But she was a light-skinned African American. For months some residents demanded her removal. But Ms. Lester was encouraged by many white classmates, her neighbors, and some school officials. To end the cross fire that tore at his daughter, her wealthy father moved her and the family to Canada.

Mary Ellen Pleasant helped slaves flee their masters in California.

Though gold rush California was largely a male place, it also attracted brave young and old women. Some packed up and left the East with their husbands or families. But women remained a rarity in the state. When some women visitors from Italy arrived, 300 Italian American men stopped panning for gold and hopefully rushed to greet them.

Though women were much in demand in the state, they still lacked equality. A daring few tried to change that. In 1855 Mary Atkins arrived in California from the Midwest to begin a Young Ladies' Seminary for "healthy, companionable, self-reliant women." Its catalog offered a rounded education.

CHAPTER 15

ON THE OREGON TRAIL

Narcissa Whitman

The route from the Missouri to the Columbia River in the Oregon Territory was first taken by European missionaries Marcus and Narcissa Whitman. They introduced it to white pioneers who started their trips from Independence, Missouri. Narcissa Whitman wrote of her 1836 trip up the Columbia: "I was never so contented and happy before. Neither have I enjoyed such health for years."

Her party traveled from six in the morning until six in the evening with a two-hour eating stop. "Tell mother I am a very good housekeeper on the prairie," she wrote.

In the 1840s both the United States and Great Britain claimed the Oregon lands between the Columbia River and the 49th Parallel. The daring of two pioneer Americans led to U.S. control of the territory. Michael Simmons, an Irish immigrant and George Washington Bush, an African American, were leaders of an expedition which headed toward Puget Sound.

Each man was reacting to oppression. Simmons resented the British telling him to keep clear of the Columbia River valley because he was of Irish lineage. Bush wanted to avoid the U.S. laws that denied people of color the right to settle in the U.S. Oregon Territory.

In 1844 the two men led a pioneer wagon caravan into British-claimed Oregon and formed a colony. The Bush family settled on land surveyed by Simmons that today is called Bush Prairie. The Bush-Simmons settlements later led to the United States claim that it, not Great Britain, owned the disputed Oregon Territory. The U.S. claim became the basis of an international agreement. U.S. control then led to the kind of black laws the Bush family had been fleeing.

However, Simmons, elected to the territorial legislature, won Bush an exemption from any

Michael T. Simmons

discrimination. In 1889 one of Bush's sons was elected to the Washington State Legislature. Another son raised a prize wheat crop.

By 1862, Chinese Americans were digging for gold in Oregon. Li Tang traveled for more than three months by land and water from San Francisco to reach the Rogue River. In his letter to his wife Mei Ling in China, he shared his many adventures:

> America is such a beautiful country. I wish you could see the wonderful things here. Many times there were no trails so we followed the rivers and streams through the mountains. We passed rivers of roaring white water and waterfalls.
> We went through forests of tall trees that almost touched the heavens. Their leaves and branches blocked the sun as we hiked through. I have seen sights you cannot see in China. Towering mountains disappearing in thick clouds. Animals that don't have names in our language. At night when we camp, we see their glowing eyes in the dark. . . .
> We bought our supplies and equipment at Sun Woo's store in a town 20 miles away from our camp. Sun Woo sold us everything on credit. We promised to pay him back when we mine enough gold. We are living in tents now, but we have to build cabins soon. Our tents aren't much use in the winter rains.

The letter Li Tang sent to Mei Ling did more than express enthusiasm and high hopes, for he had good news to share:

> We mined $35 worth of gold in the first week. With luck, in two years I may be able to return to China a wealthy man. Sometimes I think that I won't go back to China. There are nights that I dream of starting a new life here. In my dreams, I see us raising a family and running a store like Sun Woo's.

Li Tang admitted that life in America presented some unique dangers. He told of an incident with a creature he had never seen. His friend Sing Toy threw a shoe at an animal that entered his tent. It turned out to be a skunk. Li Tang described the unfolding disaster:

Ah Sam told told me that Sing Toy dashed out of his tent and jumped into the river. He said he never saw anyone run that fast before. The smell doesn't wash off with soap. Sing Toy's tent stinks so badly that we had to bury it. Everyone in camp laughed. Sing Toy didn't think it was so funny.

Colorado Gold and Nevada Silver

The pioneers, especially men, were often driven by the hope of finding precious metals that could make one an instant millionaire. The discovery of gold in Colorado in 1858 and silver in Nevada the next year, attracted eager prospectors.

Many families rode into Colorado with "Pike's Peak or Bust" signs nailed to their wagons. Some had to leave the region with new signs: "Busted, by Gosh."

But not Clara Brown. In 1859 she arrived in a wagon train when Denver was still called Cherry Creek. In an untamed land, where men out-numbered women ten to one and the law was homemade, this ex-slave decided to instill religion and order.

Brown first made her living by running a laundry. When it prospered, she turned her home into a hotel, a hospital, and a church. Her house became the first home of the St. James Methodist Church, and her generosity became a Colorado legend.

Brown's beneficiaries called her "Aunt Clara Brown" and rarely heard of her tragedies. But her early life had been marked by misfortune. At 35 her slave family — a husband, two daughters, and a son — were sold away to different owners. Finally, at 55 she had saved $100 to purchase her freedom. This was not enough, but three of her master's daughters then raised the rest of the money that was required.

Once settled and prosperous in Colorado, Brown began to search for her relatives in Virginia and Kentucky. She did not find her son or two daughters but returned with 34 other relatives and helped them settle in Denver. She finally found one daughter, Eliza Jane. Mother and daughter then continued in the Brown tradition of frontier generosity.

In Nevada, two Irish American miners, Patrick McLaughlin and Patrick O'Riley, were mystified by the "heavy black stuff" stuck to the gold they found. They had discovered silver and stumbled on the famous Comstock Lode. Their good news drew native and foreign-born miners and made boomtowns out of Virginia City, Reno, and Carson City.

In 1863 Dalmatian immigrants had started the Slavonian Gold and Silver Mining Company in Reese River. After Nevada became a state, a Slavic American, John Gregovich, was twice elected to its Senate. ■

CHAPTER 16

THE CRUSADE AGAINST SLAVERY

By the 1830s, the fight against slavery became America's most important reform effort. It united tens of thousands of men and women, rich and poor, foreign and native born, black and white. As a great democratic crusade, it touched many areas of life in the United States. Antislavery societies were the first to admit both African Americans and women to membership and promote them to leadership roles.

From the beginning of the slave trade, slaves did not accept servitude. Robbed of their freedom in Africa by European merchants, they revolted on slave ships and later on the plantations of the New World. They fled to the frontier, to Native American villages, and to whites who offered aid or liberty. Those free African Americans vigorously protested the enslavement of their brothers and sisters.

In 1808 three African American parades in New York City celebrated the law ending the slave trade. Marchers carried signs reading, "Am I Not a Man and a Brother?" In 1827 in New York City the first African American paper, *Freedom's Journal*, appeared and challenged both slavery and discrimination. It announced: "We wish to plead our own cause. Too long have others spoken for us."

Beginning in 1830, free people of color in the North held national conventions to chart their course against slavery and discrimination. But black and white antislavery people often failed to coordinate their efforts, work together, or agree on a unified antislavery program.

One man changed the debate over slavery and unified the various forces. David Walker, born free in North Carolina to a slave father and free mother, was a determined man. In 1827 he said, "I cannot remain where I must hear the chains" and left for Boston. "For the sorrows my people have suffered," he vowed revenge.

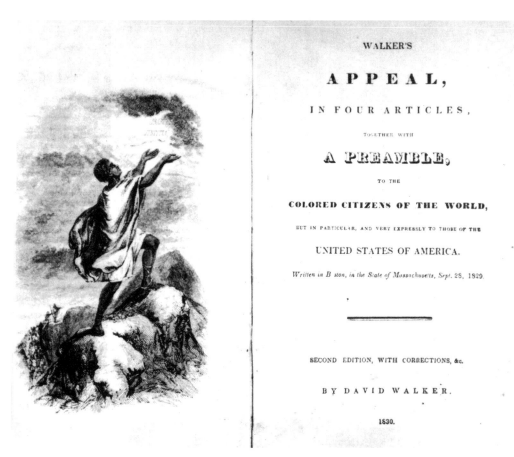

David Walker's Appeal

In Boston, Walker taught himself to read and write, and studied world history. In 1829 he published his *Appeal to the Colored Citizens of the World* which drew inspiration from the Bible, the American Revolution, and Haiti's slave rebellion. Saying "kill or be killed," Walker's *Appeal* called for a revolution by those in chains.

When the *Appeal* was read in southern cities such as Richmond, New Orleans, and Savannah, slaveholders panicked. Even opponents of slavery found its calls for a revolt disturbing. Leading white abolitionists such as William Lloyd Garrison condemned the *Appeal*.

Some abolitionists believed that owners should be paid for freeing slaves, and those liberated should be sent to another country. Walker, on the other hand, had called for immediate emancipation, no compensation, and no deportation.

In 1831 William Lloyd Garrison began his abolitionist paper, the *Liberator*. By then, Garrison agreed with Walker's approach, and he demanded an immediate end to slavery without compensation to owners or the deportation of the liberated. He wrote with the indignation of a David Walker "I will not not retreat a single inch —AND I WILL BE HEARD."

Garrison's *Liberator* called for a united, uncompromising campaign against bondage in America by whites and people of color. By this time, free Blacks had already formed 50 antislavery societies. To unify the efforts of white and black abolitionist forces, Garrison and others helped form the American Anti-Slavery Society in 1833.

African Americans were crucial to the crusade. A hundred slave escapees wrote narratives of their experiences. Ex-slaves spoke at public meetings. A rising, black educated middle class of teachers, ministers, and artisans told the general public how they felt about their sisters and brothers still in chains.

Abolitionist Frederick Douglass addresses a British audience.

Frederick Douglass, who fled his chains as a slave in Baltimore at 21, became one of the abolitionist movement's strongest voices. He published the *North Star* paper and later wrote three autobiographies. In his Rochester, New York, home, he hid runaway slaves and then helped them reach safety in Canada.

Douglass toured Europe speaking for emancipation, Irish freedom, women's rights, and world peace. Some abolitionists debated whether slaves ought to revolt to gain their liberty or whether abolitionists should take part in political campaigns. Douglass believed that African Americans should use any means necessary to achieve liberty.

C H A P T E R   17

AMERICAN WOMEN BATTLE SLAVERY

The antislavery crusade was first launched by those in chains. Men, women, and children challenged a system that held their lives in contempt.

African American women played a leading role. They first defied the rules of slavery by trying to protect their families. In Eden, Tennessee, Fannie Jennings, her daughter recalled, "fussed, fought, and kicked all the time. . . . She said she would never be whipped." "I'll kill you, gal, if you don't stand up for yourself," she told her daughter. "Fight, and if you can't fight, kick; if you can't kick, then bite."

Some slave women were able to work extra hours for "rescue" money. Thomas Jefferson's slave, Althia Tanner, saved enough money in 1810 to buy her own freedom. By 1828, she had enough cash to buy her sister, ten children and five grandchildren. In 1836 she purchased four more grandchildren. Hester Lane purchased eight adults and children and saw each child educated.

African American men and women enslaved in the South fled to the North. Then some brave souls returned to free sisters and brothers still in chains. They became part of the "Underground Railroad" in which slaves were moved from one safe "station" to another until they reached freedom in the North or Canada.

Harriet Tubman became the Underground Railroad's most daring "conductor." When she was 15 and a slave in eastern Maryland, she tried to help a man escape. Her head caught the force of a two-pound weight thrown at the man by an overseer. After that, Tubman suffered dizzy spells and sudden sleeping seizures.

In 1848 she and her husband planned an escape. When he changed his mind, she left with her two brothers. When these two young men lost heart and turned back, she reached the North alone.

In her flight from bondage, Tubman had found a new career. During the next ten years, Harriet Tubman led a series of 19 daring rescues. In her trips into Maryland's slave country, she helped 300 people escape — relatives, loved ones, and strangers.

She carried a gun in case anyone tried to stop her. She proudly said, "I never lost a single passenger." A total of $40,000 in rewards was offered for her capture dead or alive. During the Civil War, "General Tubman" returned to the South. This time she led Union soldiers on raids of liberation.

Sojourner Truth was another heroic antislavery figure. A tall, gaunt woman, she had been enslaved until New York State ended slavery in 1827.

Harriet Tubman

Then, Truth devoted her life to exposing the evils of slavery. She lectured widely, and wrote and sold copies of her own *Narrative*, an autobiography. She spent two years in Ohio on a horse-drawn wagon with 600 copies of her *Narrative* in the back. Her goal was to persuade those people who lived close to the Ohio River to aid black runaways from Kentucky and Virginia who fled across the river.

Sojourner Truth

Sojourner Truth was ready to dispute anyone who defended slavery. She also took up the cause of equal rights for women. In 1851 she confronted a man who claimed women did not need rights since they were inferior and had to be taken care of. Her response was to describe her life in bondage when nobody offered her a hand: "I have plowed, and planted, and gathered into barns, and no man could head me! And ain't I a woman?"

During the Civil War, Sojourner Truth continued with her campaigns. She met with President Lincoln to discuss emancipation. In Washington, she also tried to desegregate the city's streetcars by refusing to move out of the section designated for whites. After the Civil War, Sojourner Truth devoted her energies to the advancement of her people and of all women. "Keep the thing going while things are stirring" was her advice to women who demanded the vote.

The plight of slave women and their children stirred many white women to joint the abolitionists.

White women were deeply moved by the spirit of courageous African American women, and they were appalled by a system that denied enslaved women a Christian marriage and control of their children. From the earliest days of the antislavery crusade, white women played a leading role.

Four women were present in 1833 when William Lloyd Garrison formed the American Anti-Slavery Society. Female abolitionist societies in major cities united white women with African American women.

At first, male abolitionists asked women to raise money, collect petitions, hold bake sales, and run bazaars. They wanted to confine women to the movement's housekeeping affairs. But the determined women soon changed that.

Their inclusion in so radical a crusade created a new public climate for women and reshaped their image. In 1835 women stood together when a Boston crowd surrounded their meeting hall. The mayor refused them protection and demanded that the African American women among them be sent away. Instead, both the black women and the white women defiantly walked out in pairs, their heads held high.

When British abolitionist speaker George Thompson was attacked three times by pro-slavery mobs, American women formed a protective guard around him. The crusade against bondage had given birth to a new, determined breed of American women.

White women fought not only slavery but racism. In 1833 Lydia Maria Child, a famous children's author, wrote a pamphlet called *An Appeal in Favor of that Class of Americans Called Africans*. It was among the first writings by a white to challenge northern racism.

"It is the duty of Abolitionists to identify themselves with these oppressed Americans," Mrs. Child told a convention in 1838. She urged white women to sit next to African American women in churches, walk with them in streets, "visit them in their homes," and "receive them as we do our fellow citizens." This was a daring and unpopular position to take when most people believed Africans were inferior beings.

As the struggle over slavery intensified, women remained an important part of antislavery agitation. Some 45,000 women signed petitions denouncing the drive of slaveholders to annex Texas as a slave state. Thousands more signed petitions demanding an end to the slave trade in the nation's capital.

For espousing the cause of the enslaved, many white women endured sharp criticism from family members, ministers, and their communities. Lydia Maria Child lost her popularity as the best known author of children's books because of her forceful attacks on human bondage.

In 1852 Harriet Beecher Stowe's *Uncle Tom's Cabin* electrified the public with its tales of slavery's cruelties. To document her novel, she interviewed women and men who fled slavery. Her novel galvanized public opinion more than any other book in history. Admitted one friend, "It won more converts than a million abolitionist speeches." President Lincoln later called Mrs. Stowe "the little lady who started the big war."

Harriet Beecher Stowe

Slave owners found the book infuriating. Some were reduced to sputtering fury when it found its way into their homes and into the hands of their daughters.

The experience of publicly addressing a vital issue and daring to challenge slaveholders began to transform women. In the abolitionist movement, thousands of women first found their identity. Some vaulted over ancient barriers when they asserted their right to speak from public platforms.

Women abolitionists asserted their right to argue against men and learned how to take a public stand on political issues. Men considered these actions dangerous and revolutionary. But this only made women think more about their rights. As they fought to eliminate slavery, some began to question their own low status in society.

WOMEN: THE FIGHT FOR EQUALITY

In the first half of the 19th century, " Jacksonian Democracy" spurred a broadening of voting rights and other privileges, but these were reserved mostly for men. American women did not usually share in these changes. Wives were supposed to see themselves as inferior beings who followed the Scriptures and obeyed their fathers or husbands.

Legally, women were wards of their fathers until married, and then they became wards of their husbands. Within families, women had no rights and were treated as children. In the larger American society women could not vote, hold office, sue in court, or divorce their husbands. They had little future in business, commerce, or the professions. If a husband divorced his wife, he could keep his wife's property and their children. Elizabeth Cady Stanton, an early feminist, compared a wife to an enslaved person:

> A married woman has no legal existence; she has no more absolute rights than a slave on a southern plantation. A married women takes the name of her master, holds nothing, owns nothing, can bring no action in her own name; and the principles on which she and the slave are educated are the same. The slave is taught what is best for him to know — which is nothing; the woman is taught what is best for her to know — which is little more than nothing, man being the umpire in both cases.

Middle- and upper-class women were supposed to enjoy being ornaments — admired for their beauty, manners, housekeeping abilities, and stylish clothes. But this kind of attention, many women began to realize, was no substitute for equality.

First, women challenged an education system that was closed

to them. In 1819 Emma Willard addressed the New York Legislature. How could those kept in ignorance, she asked, become good mothers and citizens? She urged the all-male legislature to build schools for young women. In 1826 this agitation began to win allies, and Boston and New York opened high schools for girls.

Emma Willard

Colleges followed. In 1833 Oberlin College in Ohio took a step when it opened its classrooms both to young women and to African Americans. By 1853, Antioch College, also in Ohio, invited women to attend, and five years later the University of Iowa became the first public college to become coeducational.

Women had also begun to push into the teaching profession. Some started as Protestant missionaries among Native American nations, and others traveled to distant continents to convert natives. By 1835, missionary women had begun to preach among a half dozen Native American nations, in India, on the island of Ceylon, in South Africa, Sumatra, Borneo, and the Guinea coast.

Mary Lyon in 1837 opened Mount Holyoke College for young women.

So far these early gains for women had been within the realm of religion. But these missionary women served as a spur to those who felt trapped in their homes and kitchens. Some of the European religious sects that moved westward with the frontier, particularly the Baptists, Methodists, Presbyterians, and Quakers, liberalized their practices and opened doors for enterprising women.

Women living on the frontier, by taking a prominent part in church life, opened new avenues of self-expression and were able to discuss vital community issues. As early as 1829, 700 Pittsburgh, Pennsylvania, women signed petitions opposing cruel treatment of Native Americans.

For some women, the steps from religion to education to reform were short and made sense. Rebecca Gratz, born to a wealthy Philadelphia Jewish American family, devoted her life to aiding orphans and poor people. In 1819 she founded the Philadelphia Orphan Asylum. Later she was said to have begun the first Jewish American Sunday School in the United States.

In 1832 Prudence Crandall, a Connecticut teacher, opened her Canterbury Academy for Women to a young African American. White parents then removed their daughters, so Crandall enrolled

Prudence Crandall

other black teens, thirsting for a good education. Citizens of Canterbury exploded in anger. Store-owners refused to sell supplies to Crandall. Her neighbors tried to poison her well. Finally, the town government passed a law against the school and ordered her arrest. She had to close her school.

In 1851 Myrtilla Miner, a white educator, began a Washington, D.C., school to train young African American women to become teachers. Few felt the school could succeed, but it did. Her institution grew to become the famous Miner Teacher's College for Women.

Some women educators exposed other evils of society. In 1841 Dorothea Dix, a Boston teacher, began an investigation of conditions in New York, Rhode Island, and Massachusetts jails. She was shocked to find mental patients in prison, beaten as convicted criminals, and sometimes chained naked in "cages, closets, cellars, stalls, pens." Dix presented her findings to the Massachusetts State Legislature. Her crusading efforts led to the first mental hospital in New Jersey. She became a pioneer reformer of mental hospitals and a champion of humane treatment for the mentally ill.

Some women began to make their mark in the field of professional writing as reporters, authors, and editors. Sarah J. Hale was the editor of *Godey's Lady's Book,* a popular magazine for women. It was her suggestion to President Lincoln that made Thanksgiving a national holiday.

Margaret Fuller became a noted author who dared to criticize traditional male views. Women need, she said, "as a nature to grow, as an intellect to discern, as a soul to live freely and unimpeded, to

Maria Mitchell, Astronomer

Maria Mitchell was determined to pursue her career in astronomy although previously astronomy had been a field only men had entered. In 1847 as an astronomer, she dis- covered a comet that was named for her. The following year she was elected to the American Academy of Arts and Sciences, the first woman to achieve this honor. ∎

unfold such powers as were given her . . . ."

Since colonial times women had been midwives. Their experiences gave them a storehouse of medical knowledge. But medical schools did not accept women for training as doctors until Elizabeth Blackwell broke the barrier.

Some medical school officers said Blackwell was deranged for even applying. But in 1849 she graduated from a Geneva, New York, medical college. To gain her first practical experience in medicine, she had to travel to Paris. Still shunned when she returned to the United States, Blackwell and her sister opened their own hospital, the New York Infirmary for Women and Children.

Dr. Elizabeth Blackwell

Blackwell's example inspired Marie Zakrzewska in distant Poland. Zakrzewska had assisted her mother as a midwife for many years: "I learned all of life that it was possible for a human being to learn. I saw nobility in dens and meanness in palaces." In 1853 she arrived in New York and in three years graduated from Western Reserve College of Medicine.

Dr. Zakrzewska was both a pioneer woman physician and an expert in American medicine. At Blackwell's hospital she became the first resident physician.

In 1859 Dr. Zakrzewska organized the New England Hospital for Women and Children in Boston and for 40 years served as its director. She lowered another barrier when she took as one of her earliest interns Caroline Still, one of the first African Americans to enter medicine.

Dr. Zakrzewska further organized the first American school for nurses and also started the movement to build playgrounds for city children. She eagerly lent her efforts to campaigns to gain equality for women and abolish slavery in America.

Not only middle-class, educated women began to stir and to make something of their lives. Rural women also groped for ways to declare independence from their families and to escape dull farm labor.

Young farm women took jobs in early New England textile mills and soon outnumbered male employees. One, Lucy Larcum, described herself as "a naturally independent country girl" and loved the two hours of leisure time she had after her work ended. She and other factory women labored hard 12 hours a day for their

$2 a week (about a third or half of what men earned). They also had to live in carefully chaperoned boardinghouses run by the employer. But they enjoyed having their own religious life and attending nearby lectures. These activities opened a new, free world.

In Lowell, Massachusetts, factory women began a magazine, *The Lowell Offering*, edited by mill worker Harriet Farley. They wrote about the dignity of labor, the need for equality of the sexes, and of their hope to develop their talents.

The women of Lowell soon learned to stand up for themselves. In 1836 they went on strike and marched on picket lines singing,

> Oh, isn't it a pity, such a pretty girl as I,
> Should be sent to the factory to pine away and die?

When the factory owners cut their wages and increased the hours, Sarah Bagley organized the Lowell Female Labor Reform Association, an early union. Strikes became more frequent. The association collected petitions to limit the working day to ten hours and presented these to the state legislature. The young women of Lowell had boldly stepped into the area of political conflict.

Women shoemakers strike in Lynn, Massachusetts.

CHAPTER 19

THE GREAT FOREMOTHERS

The spirit of democratic reform during the Age of Jackson produced a new breed of dynamic women. Some hands that rocked the cradle were prepared to rock America's established institutions.

Frances Wright was born in Scotland in 1795 to riches but experienced tragedy early. Her father died when she was two and her mother a few years later. In 1818 she and her sister embraced American republicanism and left for New York. They traveled alone.

In a short time the sisters made friends with radical Irish refugees, traveled widely in the North and West, and loudly protested slavery. Frances became increasingly radical and wrote a play glorifying a revolt in Switzerland.

Frances developed into a tall, strikingly-attractive young woman. In defiance of custom, she wore her hair short and often was a subject of gossip. But criticism did not seem to bother her, and she kept her focus on her life's goals.

After the sisters returned to England in 1821, Fanny, as she was now called, wrote a book, *Views of Society and Manners in America* that made her famous. She and her sister joined General Lafayette in 1824 on his triumphal return tour of U.S. cities. Once again there was gossip about the two attractive young ladies who traveled with the elderly hero of the Revolution.

Fanny became interested in utopian or alternative societies founded by immigrant idealists. In Nashoba, Tennessee, she founded her own model community where former slaves and white idealists lived and interacted with each other. When her experiment failed, she saw that the ex-slaves were safely settled in the West Indies.

On July 4, 1828, Fanny Wright delivered a successful public lecture and then decided to become a platform speaker. At that time it was considered indecent for women to appear on a public platform or speak about "men's issues." But Wright welcomed the chance to be the first. The prohibition, she felt, was wrong.

Wright took on her new role with vigor. In addition to her audacity to speak in public, her words infuriated some listeners. She denounced religion, slavery, and the way society denied women education and equality. She called for the removal of all false barriers.

But Wright was bursting with even more radical ideas. She began to scoff at marriage, and she urged liberal divorce laws and advocated birth control. Families, she thought, should not have more children then they could feed. Women, she insisted, should be free to control their own lives and bodies.

For an unmarried woman to address these issues was considered sinful and an affront to community morals. But Wright's lectures were well-attended, even if they were often interrupted by angry men. Efforts were made to burn down her lecture halls.

Wright was pleased that her crowds grew and included both men and women. She began a New York paper, the *Free Enquirer*, to promote her views.

In Europe, Wright married a Frenchman after he signed a marriage contract that allowed for a simple and fair divorce. She gave birth to a daughter. In 1846 she returned to the U.S. and resumed her provocative public lectures. They became more radical.

Wright told her audiences that injustice in the world began with the earliest civilizations dominated by priest-kings whose caste systems divided people by wealth and power. Subjugation of women was, she declared, "the first master measure employed for the more certain enslavement of the species."

Audiences were still thrilled and shocked by her speeches. Some viewed her as an exotic celebrity, but others saw her as a scandalous woman seeking to undermine society.

Fanny Wright and her husband finally divorced, following the plans of their marriage contract. After an accident in Cincinnati, she died in 1852. Her daring leap onto the lecture platform had shocked most Americans and broadened the horizon of women.

Ernestine Potowski was born in 1810 to a rabbi's family in Poland. At 17 she broke with her father's religion and left his home. Four years later she was ready to take up arms for Polish indepen-

dence, but she lived in Austria at the time, and the authorities there stopped her from traveling to Poland.

In 1836 she married a watchmaker named Rose who was not Jewish, and they sailed off to rejoice in American republicanism. In New York, she witnessed her first Fourth of July celebration and called the United States a land "transformed from deformity to beauty."

But not everything pleased her. She condemned slavery as a sin against humanity and said the same about the lack of equality for women. Before there was a women's rights movement, Mrs. Rose, in her thick Polish accent, passionately demanded equality.

Upon her arrival here, she became an American political activist. In her first year she petitioned the New York State Legislature to grant married women a legal right to their property. She was among the first women to seek justice for women through the law. In 1848 after a dozen years of agitation, New York passed the first Married Women's Property Act.

As a speaker, Ernestine Rose had few equals. The brilliant abolitionist orator, Wendell Phillips, compared her eloquence to Ralph Waldo Emerson's. One entranced critic called her "the morning

Ernestine Rose (front row, second from left) at a women's rights convention.

87

glory of Poland . . . the rose of America." Other critics found her dazzling, energetic, and daring "with eyes flashing, her pale cheeks flushing, and her voice thrilling."

Mrs. Rose was unafraid to voice highly unpopular views. "The African race are not only capable of taking care of themselves," she said, "but are capable of enjoying peacefully as much liberty and as much freedom as the white man." She spoke out for free schools, women's rights, and better conditions for working people. In 1847 in South Carolina she told slaveholders of her contempt for their institution.

> The only civilization you have exists among the slaves; for
> if industry and mechanical arts are the greatest criterion of
> civilization (and I believe they are), then certainly the
> slaves are the only civilized ones among you, because they
> do all the work.

Rose charged no fee for her lectures and often paid for her audacity. In New York City in 1850 she, William Lloyd Garrison, and Frederick Douglass were punched and clubbed at a public meeting invaded by a pro-slavery mob. She was denounced as a fanatic and "Polish propagandist."

Ernestine Potowski Rose calmly answered her critics, saying she identified herself with "the downtrodden and persecuted people called the Jews." She proudly identified her broad reform interests: "I go for emancipation of all kinds — white and black, man and woman!"

Jane Swisshelm was born in 1815 in Pittsburgh to immigrant parents from Scotland. A child of the frontier, she proudly adopted its rough and raw ways. "My style I caught from the crude, rural surroundings, and was familiar with the unlearned."

Swisshelm's early life was harsh. She had to take a job at 14 when her father died and then began to teach in public schools. She loved painting. But when she married at 21, she buried this love for 20 years to concentrate on a husband who did not like her.

The young married woman found an outlet in her devotion to the Presbyterian church and in fighting slavery. During a visit to Louisville, Kentucky, she first confronted slavery. She saw a boy of 10 forced to wear an iron collar because he had run away from a leading member of the Presbyterian church. She heard a woman complain of having to send her aged, nearly blind African American cook to be publicly whipped because the white woman's husband was tired of beating the slave himself.

Swisshelm opened a Louisville school for African American children. When it was threatened with arson, she had to give it up. She returned to Pittsburgh and began to write for an antislavery paper. When it folded, she began her own journal and saw that it reached every state in the Union. Her foes, she later reported, "barked furiously . . . . A woman had started a political paper! A woman!"

Swisshelm was often sued in court for naming foes in her articles. She denounced the Mexican War for shedding "the blood of women and children." In 1850 she began to write a Washington political column for Horace Greeley's New York *Tribune*. She agitated for and won the right as a journalist to sit in the U.S. Congress' press gallery. She was never timid about demanding respect.

By 1857, Swisshelm left her husband, took her daughter, and settled in St. Cloud, Minnesota, where she began a new abolitionist paper. One of the town's most distinguished figures led a mob attack that destroyed it. Most people in St. Cloud rejected her radical views, but at a town meeting generous citizens helped raised the money for her new press.

During the Civil War, Swisshelm demanded emancipation for slaves and even met with President Lincoln on the issue. She served as a nurse and later a clerk in the War Department. As one of the first women hired for a federal war job, she again felt she had taken an "advance post on the picket line of civilization."

Margaretha Meyer, a German Jewish refugee born in 1834, did not storm at evil from lecture platforms or in newspaper columns. But she made a difference to millions in her adopted country. Meyer was a student of the famous educator Friedrich Froebel, who in 1837 in Germany established the first kindergarten. Meyer learned

Indian and African American children being instructed in a Rhode Island classroom.

from Froebel that human potential should receive early nurture and that education should rely on the untapped foundations within the individual.

With Froebel, Meyer came to believe that education, rather than being delayed until age 6 when school began, should start earlier. Froebel and Meyer romped with children in fields and devised songs, games, and activities that would encourage self-expression. Through the play of children, they were searching for ways to teach life's basic concepts.

In July 1852, Meyer was only 18 when she met 23-year-old Carl Schurz in London. Schurz was a German revolutionary, and he had fled Germany a step ahead of the police. He was taken with her "fine stature. . . . beautiful features and large, dark, truthful eyes." For both it was love at first sight. The two quickly married and in a month left for America and a new chance in life.

In Wisconsin the couple purchased a farm and soon counted themselves antislavery supporters of the new Republican Party. In 1856 Carl campaigned for Republican presidential candidate John C. Frémont and ran for office himself but lost. In their hometown of Watertown, Wisconsin, Margaretha Meyer Schurz established the first American kindergarten the same year. It was a step of lasting importance.

News of her efforts to educate children between 4 and 6 began to spread. Young Susan Blow picked up where Margaretha Schurz left off. Born in Missouri of English ancestry, Blow convinced the St. Louis superintendent of schools to incorporate kindergartens into his system. In 1873 the first public school kindergarten was started at the Des Peres School, and Susan Blow became the American "mother of the kindergarten." She went on to write three important books describing her basic theories and concepts of education.

CHAPTER 20

FROM ABOLITIONISM TO FEMINISM

It was an easy, small step for abolitionist women to realize that their restricted lives had a lot in common with slaves. Some actually were dedicated to freeing both themselves and the slaves.

One of the earliest women abolitionists was Lucretia Mott who was born in 1793. Lucretia was a Quaker and mother of six children. By her mid-20s she had become a gifted speaker for abolitionism, women's rights, temperance, and world peace. She said she preached "Truth for Authority, Not Authority for Truth." Slaves, she said, were the most oppressed people, and "I have felt bound to plead their cause." A gentle soul, Mrs. Mott summoned the tenacity and courage necessary to combat her male foes. She stood her ground in the face of derisive ministers and threatening mobs. She was a founder of the Philadelphia Female Anti-Slavery Society and served as its president for 40 years.

Mrs. Mott had a profound influence on Sarah and Angelina Grimké, sisters from a leading South Carolina political and banking family. Their slaveholding father made sure his daughters had a fine education in history, science, and languages. Later they rebelled against his views on slavery. "Slavery was a millstone about my neck and marred my comfort from the time I can remember," Sarah recalled. She secretly taught slave women to read and write. Angelina was shocked when she visited a Charleston jail where slaves were taken to be beaten.

The Grimkés became Quakers and left the South for Philadelphia. Both became great orators of the antislavery crusade. At first they only addressed friends sitting in the living rooms of abolitionist homes, but in 1837 the two sisters began a nine month antislavery speaking tour. Billed for "women only," the tour took them to 67 towns and cities. They addressed about 40,000 people, few of whom had ever heard a woman speak in public. The press denounced them for talking about "men's issues."

Men who arrived "to take my wife home" remained in the back of crowded lecture halls to listen. Then some men ventured into empty seats. With men and women sitting next to each other, the press then charged the Grimkés with addressing "promiscuous assemblies."

As the tour continued, the Grimkés turned their attention to women's rights issues, which, they explained, were linked to slavery. Sarah fired a salvo that shifted from defense to attack:

> But I ask no favor for my sex. I surrender not our claim to equality. All I ask of our brethren is that they will take their feet from off our necks and permit us to stand upright on the ground which God has designed us to occupy.

Sarah and Angelina Grimké

The Grimké's tour, said their foes, proved that abolitionists were fanatics who intended to remove the restraints that held women in place. This would unleash anarchy in the country. From the abolitionist ranks, William Lloyd Garrison, Frederick Douglass, and most other antislavery leaders upheld the right of women to be heard. But the issue caused major male defections from the cause.

Other abolitionist women began to join the Grimkés in linking the two crusades. Lucy Stone, an early abolitionist lecturer, admitted, "I was so possessed by the women's rights idea, that I scattered it in every speech."

Then in 1840, when women had been integrated into the American antislavery movement, a dramatic event occurred abroad. Lucretia Mott and Elizabeth Cady Stanton arrived as delegates to attend a London World Anti-Slavery Convention. Male officials challenged their right to be seated, and there was a floor fight. The women were expelled to the galleries. Garrison joined them in the galleries to voice his protest.

Mott and Stanton returned home with a plan to organize a special meeting on the problems men imposed on women. In 1848 at Seneca Falls, New York, they assembled a conference of 300 women and men that initiated the modern drive for equality between the sexes.

Stanton, by then a mother of seven children, drew up a resolution advocating women's suffrage. She had never spoken in public before, and when she asked her husband to introduce the resolution, he said it would "turn the proceedings into a farce." Even Mott, her lifelong friend, feared that the resolution would "make the convention ridiculous."

Stanton turned to Frederick Douglass, the former slave and eloquent abolitionist orator. Douglass agreed to second the resolution and delivered a speech urging its passage. Stanton suddenly found her own tongue. She debated those who challenged her historic resolution, and it narrowly won approval. A women's movement had been born.

Lucretia Mott (center) being escorted from a violent meeting.

FURTHER READING

Adamic, Louis. *A Nation of Nations*. New York: Harper, 1944.

Bernado, Stephanie. *The Ethnic Almanac*. New York: Dolphin, 1981.

The Council on Interracial Books for Children, ed. *Chronicles of American Indian Protest*. Greenwich, CT: Fawcett Publications, 1971.

Debo, Angie. *A History of the Indians of the United States*, rev. ed. Norman, OK: University of Oklahoma Press, 1984.

The Ethnic Chronology Series. Dobbs Ferry, NY: Oceana Publications, 1972–1990.

Evans, Sara M. *Born for Liberty: A History of Women in America*. New York: Macmillan, 1989.

Franklin, John Hope. *From Slavery to Freedom*, rev. ed. New York: Alfred A. Knopf, 1988.

Handlin, Oscar. *The Uprooted*. New York: Grosset & Dunlap, 1951.

The *In America* Series. Minneapolis, MN: Lerner Publications, 1971–1990.

Katz, William Loren. *Black Indians: A Hidden Heritage*. New York: Atheneum Publishers, 1990.

———. *Breaking the Chains: African American Slave Resistance*. New York: Atheneum Publishers, 1990.

Millstein, Beth and Bodin, Jeanne, eds. *We, the American Women; A Documentary History*, New York: Ozer Publishing, 1977.

Moquin, Wayne, ed. *A Documentary History of the Mexican Americans*. New York: Bantam, 1972.

Schlissel, Lillian *Women's Diaries of the Westward Journey*. New York: Schocken, 1982.

Seller, Maxine S. *To Seek America: A History of Ethnic Life in the United States*. New York: Ozer Publishing, 1977.

Shannon, William V. *The American Irish*. New York: Macmillan, 1964.

Thernstrom, Stephan, ed. *Harvard Encyclopedia of American Ethnic Groups*. Cambridge, MA: Harvard University Press, 1980.

INDEX

Abolitionists, 59, 74, 79, 91
Africa, 46, 47, 49
African Americans, 8, 9, 14, 17, 18, 20,
    21, 25, 43, 44, 45, 47, 48, 49-50, 51,
    56, 57, 59, 70, 81, 89
    as abolitionists, 75
    in California gold rush, 66-69
    children, 89
    free, 73
    frontiersmen, 63
    in New Orleans, 53
    in Texas, 57
    women, 78, 82
Africans, 23, 38, 40, 41, 44, 50-51, 61
African Seminoles, 40-41
Albany, New York, 36-37
American Anti-Slavery Society, 75, 78
American Revolution, 25, 40, 48, 74
American Scots, 54
Americans, 15, 19, 36
Antislavery, 76, 73
*Appeal to the Colored Citizens of the
    World*, 74
*Appeal in Favor of that Class of Americans
    Called Africans, An*, 78
Arkansas, 32
Armenian Americans, 31
Asia, 6
Asians, 56
Arizona, 60
Atlantic Ocean, 7, 10, 37
Austria, 87

Baltimore, 6, 36, 37, 45, 46, 48
Baptists, 53, 81
Bear Flag Republic, 63
Bear Flag Revolt, 21
Beth Elohim, 48
Black Laws, 9, 67
Blacks, 9, 26. See also: African
    Americans; Africans.
    Cherokees, 26
    free, 49, 55
    Indians, 26
    Seminoles, 40-42
Blackwell, Dr. Elizabeth, 83
B'nai B'rith, 8
Boone, Daniel, 20
Boston, 6, 11-12, 14, 25, 31, 36, 37, 73,
    78, 81, 82, 83
Bremer, Fredrika, 29, 46
Brumidi, Constantino, 39

Cajuns, 51, 52
California, 19, 21, 22, 60, 61-69
Canada, 75
Canterbury Academy for Women,
    81-82
Catholics, 10, 15, 33, 34, 36, 56
    Dutch, 24
    European, 33
    Irish, 13, 59

Charleston, South Carolina, 47, 48, 50
Chicago, 7, 24, 27
Child, Lydia Maria, 78, 79
Chinese, 66
    in California gold rush, 66-67
Chinese Americans, 67, 71-72
Cincinnati, 29, 30, 86
Civil War, 15, 22, 26, 28, 29, 34, 36, 47,
    48, 49, 50, 63, 67, 89
Colorado, 60
Communism, 17
Communist club, 18
Confederacy, 55
Confederate Constitution, 38
Connecticut, 26, 81
Cotton gin, 43
Crandall, Prudence, 81
Creoles, 52, 53
Croatia, 23
Croatian American, 53, 64
Cuban Americans, 24
Czech Americans, 8, 30, 56, 57-58
Czechs, 7, 8, 30, 57-58

Dalmatia, 54
Dalmatians, 54, 64
Danes, 6, 28
Danish Americans, 22, 28
Declaration of Independence, 45
Delaware, 26
Denmark, 29
De Smet, Father Pierre-Jean, 23
Detroit, 25
Dix, Dorothea, 82
Douglass, Frederick, 9, 14, 45, 59, 75,
    88, 92, 93
Dutch, 24

Emancipation, 74
England, 7, 10, 14
Erie Canal, 24, 36-37
Estonians, 6
Europe, 24, 37, 75

Feminism, 91-93
Florida, 22, 24, 40-42, 45
48ers, 17, 18
France, 31, 36, 37, 51, 52
Freethinkers, 15
Frémont, John Charles, 20, 21, 63, 90
French Americans, 54
French Canadians, 17, 19, 25
Frisians, 24
Froebel, Friedrich, 89-90
Frontier clergymen, 23
Frontiersmen, 19

Gabriel Prosser, 46-47
Garrison, William Lloyd, 74, 75, 78, 88, 92
Georgia, 41, 43, 45
German Americans, 15, 16, 17, 18, 53,
    56, 58

Germans, 15-18, 23, 31
Germany, 15, 17, 33
Gold rush of 1849, 21, 61, 62-69
Great Britain, 70
Greece, 7
Greek Americans, 54
Grimké, Angelina and Sarah,
    91-92

Hamburg, Germany, 28
Hebrew, 8, 29
Holland, 24
Houston, Sam, 56, 57
Hungarian Americans, 32, 64

Illinois, 15, 17, 25, 28
Immigrants,
    Dalmatian, 61, 72
    Danish, 27, 28
    Dutch, 24
    German, 15-18
    Hungarian, 54
    Irish, 10-14, 53, 70
    Jewish, 57
    Luxembourg, 24
    Polish, 60
    Swedish, 28
    Swiss, 24
Indian Removal Act, 32
Indiana, 15, 24, 25
Ireland, 10, 11, 13, 14, 33, 61
Irish, 11-14, 17
Irish Americans, 8, 11, 12, 13, 14, 15, 16,
    33, 34, 36, 45, 54, 59, 62, 64, 72
Italian Americans, 48, 54, 69
Italy, 31, 64

Jackson, Andrew, 32, 41, 53
Jacksonian Democracy, 80
Jacksonian Democrats, 15
Jefferson, Thomas, 48, 52, 76
Jewish Americans, 29-30, 48, 57, 64-65,
    81
    in Texas, 58
Jews, 8, 15, 29
    Polish, 32, 48
    Polish American, 49

Kearny, Stephen, 20, 21, 60
Kentuckians, 54
Kentucky, 72, 77
Know-Nothings, the 33-34

Lincoln, Abraham, 18, 59, 77, 89
Lithuanians, 63
Lone Star Republic, 57
Los Angeles, 64, 69
Louisiana, 39, 56
Louisiana Territory, 52
Louisville, Kentucky, 48
Louisville Platform, 18
Lutherans, 15, 18, 28

Marx, Karl, 17
Maryland, 26, 39, 76
Massachusetts, 26, 82
McCormick, Cyrus, 37, 38
Merrimac, the, 38
Methodist church, 23
Methodist Episcopal church, 23
Methodists, 81
Mexican Americans, 59, 60, 62, 64, 67
Mexican War, 20, 58, 59, 89
Mexicans, 57, 58, 60
Mexico, 24, 59, 60
Mexico City, 58, 60
Michigan, 23, 25
Michigan Territory, 21
Midwest, 15, 17, 28, 31, 37
Milwaukee, 7, 18, 24
Minnesota, 21, 28
Mississippi River, 21, 23, 36, 51
Missouri, 15, 35, 70
Mitchell, Maria, 82
Monitor, the, 38
Moravian mission, 23
Mormon church, 35
Mormons, 28, 35
Mott, Lucretia, 91, 93
Mountain Men, 19-23

Native Americans, 19, 21, 22, 23, 26, 30, 32, 46, 51, 52, 59, 73
  Blackfoot, 21
  in California, 61
  Chauchas, 51
  Cherokees, 26, 57
  Chickasaws, 51
  Chippewas, 21, 23, 30
  Creeks, 41
  Crow, 21
  Delawares, 23
  Huron 30
  Natchez, 51
  nations, 45, 81
  Nez Percé, 22
  Ottawas, 23
  Pottawatomie, 30
  Seminoles, 40-42
  Tejas, 56
  Wyandots, 23
  Yazoo, 51
Nevada, 60
New Brunswick, Canada, 51
New England, 9, 11, 25, 38, 39, 43
  textile mills, 83
New England Hospital for Women and Children, 83
New France, 51
New Jersey, 26, 82
New Mexico, 60
New Orleans, 6, 22, 24, 36, 37, 38, 47, 48, 51-55
New Sweden, 27
New World, 6, 44, 73
New York Central Committee of the United Trades, 17

New York City, 6, 7, 8, 10, 11, 12, 13, 16, 18, 25, 30, 31, 33, 36, 37, 51, 55, 65, 66, 73, 81, 85, 87, 88
New York State, 9, 20, 22, 25, 26, 28, 35, 82, 83
Normandy settlement, 28
North Carolina, 26, 44, 73
Norway, 26
Norwegian Americans, 26-27, 63

Ohio, 15, 24, 77, 81
Ohio River, 36, 45, 77
Oklahoma, 20, 32, 42
Old World, 8, 32
Oregon, 19, 20, 22, 70
Oregon Territory, 70

Pacific Ocean, 20, 37
Paris, France, 38, 83
Pennsylvania, 15
People of color, 49, 53, 67, 70, 75
Philadelphia, 6, 11, 12, 30, 33, 36, 39, 46, 91
Philadelphia Female Anti-Slavery Society, 91
Pittsburgh, 7, 88, 89
Poland, 87
Polish Americans, 22, 32, 60
Portugal, 8
Portuguese Americans, 54, 64
Presbyterians, 81
Protestant Americans, 18
Protestants, 13

Quakers, 26, 47, 49, 81, 91

Reform Judaism, 30, 48
Republican Party, 63
Rhode Island, 14, 82, 89
Richmond, Virginia, 28, 46, 48, 49, 74
Roberts Settlement, 26
Rochester, New York, 26, 75
Rocky Mountain Fur Company, 20
Roman Catholic church, 12

St. Louis, Missouri, 7, 17, 18, 19, 20, 48
Salt Lake City, 35
San Antonio, 56, 57
San Francisco, 61, 62, 63, 64-65, 67, 69
San Jacinto, Battle of, 57
Savannah, 48, 50, 74
Scandinavia, 29
Scandinavian American, 27
Scandinavians, 26-27
Scotland, 85
Second Seminole War, 41
Segregation, 52
Serbian Americans, 54
Slaveholders, 18, 43, 50
Slavery, 14, 45, 49, 55
  abolition of, 18
  crusade against, 73-75
  era, 46
  in the South, 43-47

Slaves, 25, 43-44, 49, 55
  families, 44
  insurrections, 46
  resistance, 41, 44, 45
  runaways, 45, 49
  trade, 73
Slavic Americans, 72
Smith, Joseph, 35
South Africa, 81
South America, 24, 63
South Carolina, 26, 88
Southwest, the, 19
Spain, 8, 51, 56
Spaniards, 53
Spanish Americans, 59
Stanton, Elizabeth Cady, 92-93
Stowe, Harriet Beecher, 79
Strauss, Levi, 65
Sutter, John, 62
Sweden, 28, 38
Swedes, 6
Swedish Americans, 27, 28
Swiss, 6, 23
Switzerland, 85

Tammany Hall, 12
Tennessee, 26
Texas, 24, 27, 28, 38, 56-60
Trail of Tears, the, 32
Truth, Sojourner, 9, 77
Tubman, Harriet, 76-77
Turner, Nat, 47

Uncle Tom's Cabin, 79
Underground Railroad, 76
United States of America, 6, 7, 8, 10-11, 14, 15, 16, 17, 24, 25, 27, 28, 29, 31, 37, 39, 46, 47, 48, 49, 51, 57, 58, 61, 70, 73, 83, 87
Utah, 28, 60

Virginia, 23, 26, 28, 72, 77

Walker, David, 73-74
War of 1812, 40
Washington, D.C., 9, 39, 48, 82
West Indies, 52, 62
Whitman, Marcus and Narcissa, 70
Willard, Emma, 81
Wisconsin, 7, 15, 25, 26, 27, 90
Women,
  American, 80
  fight for equality, 80-84
  in antislavery movement, 76-79
  voting rights for, 18
Women's movement, 93
Women's rights, 75
Wright, Frances, 85-86
Wyoming, 30, 60

Young, Brigham, 35
Yugoslav American, 23